ISBN: 979-8-9992021-0-9

First Edition

Printed in the United States of America

THE BOY IN THE ORANGE VAN

a memoir

Api Dogan

Dedication and Acknowledgments

This book is dedicated to my father, who taught me that you don't need riches to leave behind a legacy. He sold vegetables from an orange van, carried the weight of five children, and never once complained.

He showed me that dignity lives in how you carry yourself and that love, when quiet and constant, speaks louder than words. His hands were calloused, his heart was fierce, and his example still drives me every day. Everything I've built began with him. Every mile of my journey has his fingerprints on the wheel.

To my mother, whose silent strength steadied us when the world shook.

To Karla, my partner in everything, thank you for believing in me when I barely believed in myself.

To our children, who now ride in our own van, learning the stories that shaped our name.

To my siblings, friends, mentors, and strangers who lifted me—thank you.

I was the boy in the back of that van. We had little money, no map, and more reasons to give up than to keep going. But with grit, grace, and the lessons my father left behind, I built a life that spans continents, cultures, and generations. From poverty to running a multi-million-dollar enterprise—this journey is not just mine; it's his.

And to the reader holding this book:

If you're feeling lost, broken, or caught between cultures or faiths, this story is for you.

If you've drifted from your father or feel unseen by the world, this story is for you. If you're struggling to believe that you can still rise, this story is for you. If this book helps even one person find their voice, forgive their father, or believe in themselves again, that would be the greatest gift to my soul and the highest way I could honor my father's life.

With all my heart,

—Api Dogan

"He left no fortune, only an orange van and a quiet strength. We crossed continents without a map – only his memory, her love, and faith that never built walls. I carry them all: in grief, in grit, in grace. And with every mile forward, I find my way back home."

Api Dogan

CHAPTER ONE

The Beginning

I was born on April 16, 1977, in a small Dutch city called Hengelo, a place that would become the backdrop of my earliest dreams. My parents had come from a tiny mountain village in Central Anatolia, Turkey, carrying little more than grit and the hope of building a better life. They settled in a modest house in the Netherlands, and it was there—among tulip fields and cobblestone streets—that their first son was born after two daughters.

When I came into this world, a beautiful gesture of tradition met a twist of fate. My father's older brother had just returned from pilgrimage, glowing with pride and holiness, and my father, out of deep reverence, gave him the honor of naming me. My uncle, however, didn't speak Dutch. So, when he softly whispered "Apturrahim" to the nurse, she struggled to understand. Her hand scribbled the closest thing she could manage: "Apiturahim."

A mistake? Maybe. But it would become my name. Api.

At first, it was just what people called me. But over time, it became something more—a name that came to represent resilience, adaptation, and the quiet poetry of life taking its own course. It wasn't what I was supposed to be called, but it was what I became. It stayed with me through every joy, sorrow, and mile of the journey that lay ahead.

Api was the boy who watched his father with adoration, who learned from the land of windmills and waffles how to laugh with his whole heart. Api was the boy in the orange van.

And one day, that name—born from a misunderstanding—would echo across boardrooms, airports, highways, and continents because it wasn't just a name. It was the beginning of a story.

Hengelo

To most people, Hengelo was just a quiet Dutch town near the German border. But to me, a 9-year-old boy bursting with wonder, it was a magical land that seemed to exist just for me. Every street, every breeze, every creaking gate felt like it held a secret waiting to be discovered.

I remember the windmills—tall and noble—dotting the horizon like ancient guardians. Their blades turned slowly, rhythmically, as if waving to the sky. I'd ride my little bike past them, feeling like I was pedaling through a painting. The farmlands were endless stretches of green and gold, brushed with patches of wildflowers. And the cows—those black-and-white cows—stood so still they looked like they had been carefully painted into place.

Sometimes, my father would take us to nearby farms to buy fresh milk and eggs. I remember the farmer tipping a glass bottle under the metal spout, the milk rushing out warm and frothy. We'd leave with our hands full and our hearts fuller. Those were quiet moments, but they planted something inside me: an appreciation for simplicity, for the earth, for things made with care.

The streets of Hengelo were cobblestone, uneven under my shoes, and lined with little boutique shops that felt like treasure chests. The butcher always gave me a wink and a slice of sausage. The baker knew our names. There was something about that neighborhood that made you feel seen.

But nothing—nothing—made my heart race like Patat. Thick, golden fries topped with diced onions, sweet ketchup, and creamy mayonnaise, served in paper cones. I'd bite into them with both hands, my face smeared with sauce, my eyes wide with joy. It was my favorite meal in the world, and somehow, it tasted even better when shared with my sisters, sitting on a wooden bench with the breeze tousling our hair.

And then there was drop—black licorice. A candy so bold and strange that it divided people into lovers and haters. I was firmly in the lovers' camp. I'd let it sit in my mouth, savoring the strong flavor as I watched bikes glide by on the brick road.

Springtime in Hengelo brought an explosion of color. Tulips in every shade—red like joy, yellow like sunlight, purple like secrets. My sisters and I would pick them from our yard and place them carefully in small glass jars on the windowsill.

And when summer came, Hengelo transformed into a wonderland.

There were festivals in the town square—music, games, food, laughter. But nothing matched the enchantment of the Carnaval. I remember walking under the strings of lights that blinked like stars. Rides spun and soared, cotton candy floated in clouds, and music echoed into the night. I'd hold my father's hand tightly, never wanting to let go, never wanting that night to end.

Looking back, Hengelo wasn't just the place where I grew up.

It was the place where I first learned how beautiful life could be.

The House

Our house at 38, Elisabeth Street wasn't grand. It wasn't large or fancy. But to me, it was a castle. It was the safest place in the world—the place where laughter echoed through the walls and where I felt like the luckiest boy alive.

It stood modestly on a quiet street, its two-story frame made of dark red brick, maybe closer to brown when the rain fell. The front yard was small but pristine, bordered by hip-high bushes trimmed with loving precision. A wooden gate creaked when opened, and that sound, even now, feels like home. Across the narrow street, a small creek trickled gently, its song a soft, comforting backdrop to our lives.

The large window in the living room looked out over that creek. I would often press my forehead to the glass and just… watch. Ducks paddling by. Leaves drifting across the water. The world felt peaceful, and I felt like I was in the center of it.

Inside, the house was cozy. The main room was our heart—where we gathered, where we laughed. It led into a small dining area and an even smaller kitchen. But in my mother's hands, that kitchen worked miracles. The smells that came from it—fresh bread, simmering soups, frying onions—are etched into my soul. I didn't need an alarm clock. The scent of food and the soft sound of my mother's footsteps in the kitchen woke me every morning like a lullaby in reverse.

From the kitchen, a back door opened to a larger backyard. That yard was wild and alive. My mother had carved out a garden there, growing herbs and vegetables we used in our daily meals. Mint, parsley, tomatoes, peppers, they weren't just food. They were love, sprouting from the earth by her touch.

A narrow staircase led to the second floor, where three bedrooms held all our dreams. My parents' room, my sisters' room, and a small one I shared with my younger brother. That room was our universe. We turned it into forts, spaceships, and racetracks. We whispered secrets beneath our blankets and giggled until we fell asleep.

But what I remember most… is my father's ritual.

Every morning, before the sun rose and the first bird dared to sing, my father would slip quietly into each room. He would lean over each of us, kiss our foreheads gently, and leave for work. He never missed a day. Not once. Those kisses were more than habit—they were his way of saying, I'm here. I'm working for you. I love you.

That house breathed with love. It smelled of fresh food and clean laundry. It echoed with Turkish lullabies and Dutch schoolbooks. It pulsed with the gentle rhythm of a family that had little but felt like it had everything.

Even now, when I wake to the smell of something baking, I close my eyes, and I'm back there. I'm home. I'm 9 years old, and my mother is in the kitchen, and my father is lacing his boots in the hallway.

It was more than just a house.

It was the first place I ever felt joy. It was the first place I ever felt safe. And it was the last place that felt whole—before the world started to change.

The Orange Van

If my childhood had a soul, it would be painted orange, with square headlights and the steady rumble of a diesel engine. My father's old Volkswagen van wasn't just transportation. It was our companion. Our adventure machine. Our second home. Our treasure chest of memories on wheels.

It stood out like a bright ember on Elisabeth Street—bold, boxy, and unforgettable. Even in a quiet Dutch neighborhood, everyone knew whose van it was. That orange beast had character. It was never just a vehicle; it was my father's pride and joy. And over time, it became mine too.

The inside smelled like leather, dust, and fresh bread, depending on the day. The front dash held an old-style radio with a cassette player, which felt like a spaceship control panel to me. The knobs were stiff, and the volume dial had a click that was deeply satisfying. My father would slide in a cassette of Turkish folk songs and let the van fill with melodies that told stories of longing, love, and home. Sometimes, he would hum along softly. Other times, when the mood struck, he would sing out loud, and my mother, sitting beside him, would join in. Their voices dancing together felt like a secret only we knew.

The back of the van had rows of seats that my father would remove before long trips. He transformed that space into a nest for us— blankets, pillows, snacks tucked into corners, little toys rolling around the floor. It was cozy chaos, the kind that made you feel like you belonged somewhere special.

But it wasn't just the comfort. It was what the van represented.

That van took us everywhere. Every summer, it carried us on a magical journey across Europe, from Hengelo to the heart of

Turkey. We'd pass windmills, alpine mountains, sunflower fields, and shepherds waving from the hillsides. It was our moving fortress, protecting us from the unknown while showing us the world.

But it wasn't just for vacations. The van worked as hard as my father did.

On weekends, it was a produce truck—loaded with tomatoes, cucumbers, and peppers—crossing into Germany for the farmers markets. And on evenings when the rest of the world was resting, my father would fill it with warm pastries from the bakery and park it outside concerts and events, selling them one by one to the crowd. The van smelled like fresh dough and determination.

It was more than a way to make money. It was a lesson in resilience.

My father never complained. He never said he was tired. He just did what needed to be done with quiet pride and unstoppable drive. He was teaching us, without saying a word, what it meant to hustle with dignity. That orange van wasn't just part of the job—it was part of the dream. Every crate of vegetables and every roll of pastry was one step closer to the future he was building: a hotel and a gas station in Sarıkaya, his dream town back in Turkey.

To me, the van felt like an extension of my father himself. Reliable. Constant. Strong. It showed up every day, no matter the weather, no matter how tired it was. And so did he.

Even now, decades later, every time I see a van like that on the road, I point and say to my wife and kids, "That's the van. That's my van." And for a second, I'm back there again, sitting behind the driver's seat, the road stretching out before us, my father humming a tune, and everything I ever loved packed inside that orange box on wheels.

As long as I remember that van, I remember him. The smell, the sounds, the strength. It was never just metal and rubber. It was my childhood. It was my father's heart. It was home.

The Path to School in Hengelo

Every morning in Hengelo began with a small ritual that now lives in my heart like a dream I never want to wake from. I'd walk to school with my two older sisters, hand in hand, and our jackets zipped up against the cool Dutch air, our shoes crunching softly along the tidy sidewalks. Sometimes, we took our bikes — me pedaling fast to keep up with their longer legs — other times, we simply strolled, savoring the peaceful rhythm of our routine.

Part of the path ran along a narrow, gentle creek right in front of our house. The water sparkled in the early light, and ducks would often waddle by or float lazily along the banks. Then we'd cut behind rows of homes with immaculate gardens. Each garden offered a new delight — the perfume of roses, the sharp green scent of hedges, the sweetness of freshly turned soil. It was like walking through a corridor of nature's blessings.

One of my favorite parts of the walk was passing the neighborhood bakery. The scent of freshly baked bread and pastries wafted out through the vents and open windows, hugging the path like an invisible welcome. Warm, yeasty, and sweet — that smell could lift your heart before the day had even begun. I'd breathe it in deeply, letting it fill me with quiet joy.

Our school itself felt like a magical kingdom to me. The building was modern but warm, with large windows that flooded the classrooms with natural light. Inside, everything felt colorful, soft, and safe. Each class had only 15 to 20 children, so it never felt crowded or noisy. The teachers spoke gently, with encouragement in their voices and patience in their eyes. They never yelled, only guided.

Outside, the playground was filled with laughter. We had everything a child could dream of: a wide-open soccer field, a basketball court, a volleyball area, and even a swimming pool — something few schools had. There was a large gymnasium with high ceilings where we played games and learned how to move with confidence and joy. Everything about that school invited us to explore, to learn, and to simply be children.

By the time I reached my classroom each morning, I felt amazing, light, excited, alive. That walk, those smells, the cheerful chatter in Dutch or Turkish between me and my sisters, it all blended into a melody of happiness. We felt so safe, so deeply content.

And sometimes, on our way home, I would let my sisters go ahead. I'd stop at one of the wooden benches along the path, nestled under a tree or beside the creek. I'd sit there in silence, listening to the birds, watching the wind play with the leaves, and inhaling the wonderful smells of flowers, fresh bread, and life. In those moments, I felt a quiet kind of joy that even now brings tears to my eyes because I know what it meant to feel truly free, truly safe, and deeply loved.

The Clay House

It was just an ordinary lump of earth unnoticed by most. But in my hands, it became something more.

I don't remember exactly where I found the clay—maybe near the creek across our street or in a neighbor's garden, but I remember how it felt cool, malleable, and inviting. I sat quietly in the backyard of our home on Elisabeth Street, away from the noise of my siblings, and started shaping it with my small, determined fingers.

Walls. A roof. A doorway. A few tiny windows pressed in with the tip of a stick. It wasn't much bigger than my hand and certainly not symmetrical. But to me, it was perfect. It was a house—a whole world that I had created out of nothing.

When my father came home from work that day—dusty, tired, with his shirt collar damp from sweat—I ran to him, holding it out with pride. "Baba, look what I made!"

He knelt slowly, took it into his strong hands, and turned it over gently. He didn't say much at first. He just studied it like it was a delicate artifact. Then he looked at me with eyes full of light and said, "My son… you're going to be a builder. A creator. One day, you'll make things the world will talk about."

I didn't know what that meant, not fully. I was just a boy who loved to play in the dirt. But in that moment, I saw something in his eyes that stayed with me for life: belief. Pure, proud, unshakable belief.

He didn't toss it aside or let it get lost in the clutter. He placed it on a little shelf in the corner of our living room, right beside the small vase of plastic flowers and a few framed photos of family back in Turkey. And every time someone visited, he'd proudly point to it:

"Look what my son made. With his own hands. He's going to do big things."

At the time, I thought he was just being kind. But now I know it was his way of planting a seed in me. He saw something long before I did.

That clay house wasn't just child's play. It was my first creation. It was the moment I learned that something didn't have to exist until I imagined it. And that I had the power to take an idea and give it form.

Years later, when I found myself in a new country with nothing but grit and dreams, I would return to that memory. When I started building a business in an industry that had long resisted change, I remembered the clay. The shape. The vision. The belief. And I built something real. Something that lasted.

That little clay house was my father's first investment—not in money, but in confidence. And it taught me something I now pass on to my own children:

You don't need permission to create. You just need the courage to begin, the patience to build, and someone who believes in you before the world does.

And for me, that someone was my father.

The Race

It was a quiet afternoon in Hengelo, the kind where the breeze carried hints of spring and the world felt gentle. My father, on one of his rare free days, suggested we all go to the park, just me and my two older sisters.

We walked the few blocks to a park near our house, where a looping trail was wrapped around clusters of trees and patches of wildflowers. As we arrived, my father looked at us with a twinkle in his eye, the kind of playful spark that always meant something special was about to happen.

"Let's have a race," he said, smiling. "Whoever finishes first gets twenty-five cents."

To a nine-year-old boy, that wasn't just money; it was a treasure. It meant a trip to the candy shop or a bag of patat with extra onions and mayo. But more than that, it meant a chance to shine, to make my father proud.

He lined us up at the edge of the path, one hand raised in the air like a referee. "Ready… set… go!"

I took off like a bullet. My legs pumped furiously, my heart thundered, and the world around me blurred. I didn't look back. I didn't slow down. I just ran—toward the finish line, toward my father's arms, toward that feeling I chased more than anything: his pride.

And I won.

Breathless and glowing with joy, I jumped into his arms. He lifted me up, spun me around, and handed me the coin. "You did it, Api!" he said, beaming. "You earned it!"

I believed I had outrun everyone with sheer determination.

But years later, long after my father had passed, my sisters shared a quiet truth: he had asked them to hold back. He had whispered to them to let me win.

Because he knew.

He knew he was sick. He knew his days of playing, running, and laughing with us were running out. He wanted—just once—to see his only son win. To see me radiant, proud, and full of life. That race wasn't for me. It was for him.

And now, when I look back, I understand.

He gave me a memory that would carry me through grief. He gave me a lesson I would one day pass on to my own children:

Sometimes, love means stepping back so someone else can fly. Sometimes, it means giving without being noticed, creating joy while standing in the shadow.

That twenty-five-cent coin is long gone. But that fierce, selfless love of a father who wanted one more perfect moment with his son remains. Forever.

Road Trip

Every summer, when the school year finally came to an end, something magical began: the great road trip from Hengelo to my mother's village in Central Anatolia. It was more than a vacation; it was a ritual, a passage, a celebration of everything we were as a family. And at the center of it all was our faithful and familiar orange Volkswagen van, filled with love.

My father would begin preparations days in advance. The back seats of the van were removed with care, making room for what would become our traveling nest. My mother would lay down thick blankets and soft pillows, transforming the space into a cozy haven for her five children. She tucked snacks and small surprises into corners, and even the way she packed felt like a quiet act of love.

We'd set off early, just after dawn. The sun would rise behind us as we left the quiet streets of Hengelo, and with every passing hour, the world outside our windows began to change. Through the Netherlands, into Germany, Austria, Yugoslavia, Bulgaria, and finally Turkey—the landscapes melted one into another like scenes from a dream.

The road was long, but it never felt that way. We'd stop often, not just for fuel or rest, but to live—in grassy fields, under leafy trees, near flowing rivers. My mom would unpack homemade sandwiches: thick slices of bread with cheese, olives, tomatoes, cucumbers, and a dusting of salt. She'd hand out cookies from tin containers and pour tea from a thermos. These weren't just meals; they were picnics with laughter, shared stories, and my father humming quietly in the background.

There was always music.

My father would slide a cassette into the van's player—old Turkish songs full of longing and memory. He'd sing softly, the rhythm of his voice keeping time with the tires on the road. Sometimes, my mother would join him, her voice light and warm. As a child, I didn't always appreciate those songs. They were slow, emotional, and heavy in a way I didn't understand. But now, as a man, I can't drive without them. They are woven into my soul. When I play them on road trips with my own children, I feel my father's presence beside me, singing through the speakers.

The moment we crossed the Bosphorus Bridge in Istanbul—from Europe into Asia—I felt a shift. This was the symbolic line between the life we knew and the life we came from. The skyline blurred past, and the van moved forward through winding hills, sunflower fields, and dusty roads that finally led to my mother's village. We were home, yet we were not. We belonged to both worlds, and the orange van knew the way to each.

And then, there was that year.

We had stopped at a fuel station somewhere between Austria and Yugoslavia. My baby brother was asleep in the back, and my mother had taken me and my sisters to the restroom. My younger brother—still a toddler—slipped away unnoticed, following behind us.

My father, assuming everyone was accounted for, fueled up and drove away.

It wasn't until we were deep into the drive that my father began calling out our names. One by one, we answered until one name echoed back in silence.

Panic. My mother's scream. My sisters were crying. My father's face drained of all color as he spun the van around and raced back faster than I'd ever seen him drive.

When we reached the station, there he was—our little brother— sitting with strangers, eating a cookie, surrounded by kindness. He ran into our arms, laughing. But when my father saw him, he did something I had never seen before: he cried.

Real tears. Silent. Trembling.

That day, I saw that even the strongest man I knew was vulnerable to love. His tears taught me that strength doesn't mean never breaking. It means loving so deeply that the thought of loss becomes unbearable.

That van didn't just carry our bodies. It carried our lives. Our fears. Our hope. Our love.

To this day, when I take my own children on road trips, I recreate it all. I pack the sandwiches, play the same music, and tell the same stories. I tell them about the orange van and their grandfather. And every time, I whisper to myself:

"Everything that mattered in my world was once held together inside that orange van."

The Farmers Market

My father worked full-time at a leather factory in Hengelo, where sheep skins were treated, dyed, and shaped into clothing. It was a tough job, physically demanding and pungent with the sharp scent of chemicals and raw hides. But to him, it was honorable work. He never came home complaining. Instead, he came home with his sleeves rolled up, kissed each of us on the forehead, and asked, "How was school today?"

But for my father, full-time work was never enough. He was a dreamer, and dreams don't wait for weekends.

Every Saturday and Sunday, he would rise before the sun and turn our beloved orange van into a mobile market stall. He'd load it with crates of the freshest produce from nearby farms—red tomatoes still warm from their source shiny eggplants, crisp cucumbers, and bundles of herbs that filled the van with their aroma. With me at his side, he'd drive across the border into Germany, where the big farmers markets bustled with life.

I loved those trips. We'd arrive early and set up our stand, laying out the vegetables in neat rows, brushing off dirt, and stacking crates like towers of color. Then, the dance began. My father would call out in Turkish-accented German, smiling wide and handing out samples. And I'd copy him—loud, energetic, my tiny voice echoing through the crowd:

"Come and try! Fresh from the farm! You won't find better!"

He'd laugh and say, "Let's see who sells more today." I always tried to beat him. Sometimes I did. But it wasn't about competition. It was about learning.

Without knowing it, I was learning how to talk to strangers, how to present myself, how to sell something with pride, and how to work for what I wanted. And more than anything, I was learning by watching a man who never sat still, never made excuses, and always made it look like love.

But the work didn't end when the sun went down.

In the evenings, especially when there were concerts, weddings, or big community events, he'd visit local bakeries and buy trays of warm pastries—simit rings, sweet rolls, puffed dough filled with cheese or olives. He'd fill the van with those scents—soft and golden, like the inside of a bakery oven—and park outside event venues. People came pouring out, hungry after dancing or praying or celebrating. My father would be there, smiling, selling.

Even when the money came slowly, he never showed frustration. He folded each coin, each bill, with respect. Every cent he earned was a step closer to something bigger.

Because he had a plan.

He wasn't just working for survival. He was building toward a dream: to return to Turkey one day and build an apart-hotel and gas station in a town called Sarıkaya—about an hour from the small village where he was born. To anyone else, that might have sounded like fantasy. But to my father, it was a promise he made to himself every time he wiped the sweat from his brow.

He worked like a man planting seeds in rocky soil—believing something beautiful would grow. And I watched him. I watched the way he kept going when others rested. I saw his pride when we sold out our crates. I saw his joy when I handed him a fistful of coins from my sales and said, "Look, Baba, I did it."

That van wasn't just our vehicle. It was his office. His stage. His temple. And every market day, every night under neon lights and pastry wrappers, there was another lesson:

That success doesn't come from luck. It comes from waking up early, showing up fully, and never giving up on the dream only you can see.

Leaving Me Behind

Not every market weekend came with laughter.

There was one morning that quietly and deeply broke something in me.

The orange van was rumbling outside, ready to head for the German farmers' market. I had already washed my face, put on my little jacket, and was bouncing with excitement. I loved these trips. I loved being with my father, standing tall beside him, pretending I was as grown as he was.

But something was different that day. My sisters were whispering in the hallway. My mother kept glancing at the door. Then suddenly, I heard the sound I never wanted to hear: the van starting.

Confused, I ran outside barefoot, just in time to see it slowly pull away from the curb.

In the backseat, through the small window, my sisters waved. One of them yelled my name.

"Api!"

I ran after the van. Fast. Faster than I'd ever run before. My legs stretched, my chest burned, and my heart pounded like a war drum. But it was too late. The orange van was gone, swallowed by the morning fog and my father's decision.

I collapsed in my mother's arms, sobbing.

Why them? Why not me?

I felt forgotten, rejected, small. It wasn't just about the market but about missing a day with him. A whole day in his presence. A whole day of being called "my little helper." That morning, it felt like I had been left behind, not just from the van but from his heart.

My mother held me and tried to soothe me. "Next time," she whispered. But the sting didn't go away.

I cried for hours.

Later, I would learn it wasn't favoritism. My father had simply wanted to rotate who joined him. Give my sisters a turn. Let them feel the pride of working by his side, too. It was fair.

But to a child—fair doesn't ease the pain.

Still, even in that pain, there was a lesson. A hard one. One that took me years to understand:

Sometimes in life, you will be passed by. You'll watch others ride ahead while you're left standing still. And it will hurt. But your worth isn't decided by one missed opportunity. It's decided by how you get up, how you carry your love forward, and how you wait for your turn with grace.

I forgave my father. Not right away. But in time. And now, whenever I think of that day, I remember the ache, but I also remember what it taught me.

That love doesn't always come dressed in understanding. Sometimes, it rides away in an orange van... only to return in different forms.

The Tree Climbing

It was the eve of Eid, and joy was bubbling through every corner of our house. We had just returned from the farmers' market, and our home was alive with the smells of lamb stew, simmering vegetables, and pastries dusted with powdered sugar. My mother was everywhere at once—stirring, chopping, bathing us one by one, then carefully dressing us in our freshly pressed Eid clothes.

I still remember the feel of that outfit—crisp navy dress pants and a white button-down shirt. It wasn't just clothing; it was a celebration. It meant something big and beautiful was coming.

Our cousins arrived, and the house was filled with the kind of chaos only big Turkish families could create—laughter, stories, teasing, and plates passed from hand to hand. My mother had outdone herself. The table was a masterpiece. The joy was thick in the air, like something we could scoop up and eat with our hands.

And then, after dinner, we ran outside.

We were a gang of six—me, my siblings, and our cousins—united in mischief and wonder. Behind our house stood an old, towering tree. Its branches stretched wide and strong, like the arms of a giant inviting us upward. Without thinking twice, we climbed.

Higher and higher we went until we could see the rooftops of the neighborhood, the glowing windows of homes filled with families just like ours. The sun was beginning to set, washing the sky in gold and rose. For a moment, we were kings and queens of the world—free, wild, full of life.

But joy has a way of turning quickly.

When we climbed down, our new Eid clothes were ruined—streaked with sticky green sap and bits of torn bark. We looked at each other in horror. Our mother's hard work. Her pride. All of it was undone by one wild climb.

When we walked in, my mother saw us and gasped.

Tears welled in her eyes. She had worked so hard, and in one afternoon, we had shattered the picture-perfect memory she had tried to create. She wasn't just angry. She was heartbroken.

Then came the sound of the front door opening. My father stepped in.

He looked at our stained clothes, at my mother's devastated face, and his jaw tightened. Without a word, he lined us all up in the living room. In his hand was a wooden spoon. My cousins began trembling. My heart was pounding.

"I want you all to learn a lesson," he said.

He started with the cousins, giving each of them a light tap. But the drama of the moment made their screams exaggerated, theatrical, and loud. "Ouch! Owww!"

And then it was my turn.

He looked into my eyes and gave me the smallest smile. And leaned down.

"Just scream," he whispered.

He tapped me so gently that I barely felt it.

"Owwww!" I yelled, playing my part.

But inside—I melted.

That moment was one of the clearest examples of my father's love. He didn't spare me because I was his favorite. He spared me because he understood something deeper: that love can teach without shaming and that discipline can come with mercy.

He wanted the other kids to think he had treated us all equally. But he gave me a secret only I would carry.

From him, I learned that being strong doesn't mean being harsh. True strength is knowing when to be soft. True leadership is protecting someone's dignity, even when you're teaching them a lesson.

That night, I went to sleep still wearing my stained shirt, the sap crusted into the seams. But my heart? My heart was clean, glowing with love. My father had taught me something without saying a word.

He didn't need to raise his voice to raise a man.

These Bright Days: Eid and Christmas

There are certain memories so vibrant, so golden, that they shine even through the darkest chapters of life. For me, those were the holidays—Eid and Christmas. Two worlds, two celebrations, but both filled with the same warmth: family, food, and the quiet magic my father and mother created for us.

Eid was electric. The night before, our home would transform. My mother moved like a whirlwind—ironing clothes, baking sweets, boiling syrup for pastries that filled every room with the scent of joy. She'd comb our hair and lay out our outfits at the foot of our beds. My sisters and I would hardly sleep, our excitement bubbling like the tea in her pot.

Morning came early. We'd jump into our new clothes—mine always a little too stiff, the shoes always a little too shiny. My father would line us up and gently inspect us like a proud commander sending his troops into joy. Then we'd pile into the orange van, hearts racing.

At the local community hall, we met other Turkish families— fathers in pressed suits, mothers in sparkling scarves, and children with wide, sugared smiles. There were balloons, little plastic toys, and magic shows. One year, there was even a clown. I remember holding my father's hand so tightly while we watched the magician pull ribbons from his sleeve. I wasn't sure if the magic was on stage... or standing right beside me.

But just as dear to me as Eid was Christmas.

People are often surprised when I tell them that. "You're Muslim; how could you love Christmas?" But to a child growing up in Hengelo, Christmas wasn't just a Christian holiday. It was a season of beauty, belonging, and wonder.

The streets lit up in soft, golden strings of light. Stores transformed their windows into tiny snow-covered villages. Music played everywhere—"Jingle Bells" in Dutch, "Stille Nacht" with its hushed reverence. I sang every word. In school, we'd make snowflakes from white paper and tape them to the windows. We'd draw Santa and his reindeer; the halls smelled of cinnamon and crayons.

And then came Christmas Eve.

My siblings and I would place glasses of milk and a few cookies by the door. We didn't have a fireplace, so we left our shoes out instead. "Santa will come in through the window," we whispered to each other, full of belief.

What we didn't know and wouldn't learn until much later was that Santa was our father.

While we slept, he would quietly tip the glasses just enough to make it look like Santa had taken a sip. He'd crumble the cookies, smudge the plate, and—somehow—place little toys into each of our shoes. Not expensive ones, but thoughtful ones. A small doll, a toy car, a spinning top.

He never told us it was him. He never wanted credit. He simply watched from the hallway the next morning as our eyes lit up, pretending to be surprised.

That was my father's kind of magic—the invisible kind. The kind that asked for nothing in return but gave you everything.

I loved Eid for its drums, pastries, and Turkish joy. I loved Christmas for its quiet wonder, its glowing lights, and the way my Dutch friends welcomed me as one of their own. But more than anything, I loved the way my father made me feel like both holidays were mine—that I belonged to something larger, something beautiful on both sides.

He never drew a line between our roots and the world around us. He made us feel that we could live in two cultures—not torn but enriched. And that's a gift I still carry: to embrace all that you are, without apology.

Even now, when the holidays come around, I hear his voice in the laughter of my children. I see his quiet smile in the glint of string lights. And I try—imperfectly but earnestly—to create that same magic he once created for me.

He made joy feel like home.

Arrival of the Baby

It was one of the most unforgettable days of my childhood, the day our baby brother came home.

My younger brother was too small to remember it now, but I wasn't. Neither were my two older sisters. The excitement in our house that day was electric. We hadn't seen the baby yet, only heard whispers of how tiny he was, how soft, and how beautiful. I had spent the whole night dreaming about his face, his cry, what it would feel like to finally become his big brother.

The three of us stood by the large glass window in the main room, eyes fixed on the street, hearts pounding like drums. Every car that passed made us jump.

And then… I saw it.

That bright orange Volkswagen van, like a beacon of joy, turned into our street.

I screamed, "They're here! They're here!" My sisters joined me in a rush of squeals, and we bolted for the door, tripping over ourselves in our urgency. We flung it open, ran down the path, flung open the little wooden gate, and ran into the street.

As my father pulled the van to a stop, the air felt like it had paused—like time itself was holding its breath.

We yanked open the side door, breathless.

And there he was.

Our baby brother… was wrapped in a soft blue blanket and tucked gently into my mother's arms. He was pale and perfect, still and glowing like an angel. I reached out instinctively, aching to hold him. But my mother smiled and said gently, "Just look, Api. Not yet."

So, I looked.

And for a moment I can still feel in my bones, I saw something holy. As my mother stepped out of the van with him in her arms, it was as if an angel had emerged from that orange chariot. The street faded. The sounds of the world melted away. All I saw was light, life, and love.

That van… that orange van… it wasn't just a vehicle. It was a cradle of memories. It brought home vegetables. It brought us to weddings. It brought us joy.

But on that day, it brought home something divine.

From that moment, I understood something: life is not made up of years; it's made up of moments. And some moments come wrapped in blue blankets, carried in the arms of your mother, stepping out of a van driven by the man who means everything to you.

That image never left me.

And it never will.

The Swimming Pool

It was supposed to be an ordinary summer day, the kind filled with light and laughter. My two sisters had been invited to a birthday outing at a swimming pool—one of those exciting places with fountains and twisting slides that seemed to touch the sky. I had been there once before, on a magical trip with my father in the orange van. The memory was still fresh—how my feet had danced on the warm tiles, how the water had made me feel like I was flying.

But this time, I wasn't invited.

My sisters were going with friends, biking there on their own. I was supposed to stay home. My mother had other things to do and trusted me to remain behind. But something in me refused to be left out. Maybe it was curiosity, maybe a craving to be included. But mostly, it was the ache of not being part of their world. I waited until they had gone, then slipped out the back on my bike and quietly followed them.

The pool came into view, glittering in the sun like a field of diamonds. My heart pounded with anticipation. But when I got to the gate, I was stopped cold. I wasn't on the list. I had no money for a ticket. No invitation. No way in.

So, I stood there—hands gripping the iron fence—watching from the outside.

I could see them playing. Laughing. Splashing. My younger sister kept glancing back at me with guilt in her eyes. But my older sister… she looked away. She ignored me. And that pierced deeper than any locked gate.

The sun began to fade, and with it came something darker. Clouds rolled in quickly. The wind picked up. Thunder growled low and long. Suddenly, the fun stopped. Whistles blew. Staff rushed to evacuate the pool. A storm was coming.

As the first drops of rain fell, we mounted our bikes and began the ride home. But it wasn't just rain; it was a tempest. The wind howled in our ears, and lightning flashed like angry veins across the sky. At one point, the wind was so strong that I didn't even need to pedal. I was flying forward on sheer force, soaked to the bone, my eyes stinging with water and fear.

Then with a crack of thunder, a tree crashed down across the street just ahead. We were stranded. Shivering. Crying.

Out of nowhere, an elderly man waved at us from his porch. He ushered us into his warm home and gave us towels, hot milk, and cookies. For a moment, we were safe. But back at home, chaos had erupted.

My father had come home to an empty house. No wife. No children. No Api.

He jumped into the orange van, driving through the storm, street by street, calling our names into the roaring wind.

When the storm finally calmed, we made it home—soaked, cold, but safe.

My mother ran to us, her face lined with relief and fear. "Go to bed," she whispered. "Pretend to be asleep. Your father... he's very upset."

I climbed into bed, heart pounding like thunder. My window faced the street. And then I saw it—that orange van, wet and glistening, pulling into our driveway like a returning hero. But for the first time, I wasn't happy to see it.

My father stormed into the house. I heard his voice—angry, rising with fear. "Where are they?!" My mother whispered something calming. Footsteps came down the hall. My bedroom door creaked open.

He looked at me, lying there "asleep," my clothes still damp, my lashes still wet with tears.

And then he said to my mother, with a sigh that broke something inside me:

"They're lucky they're asleep. They just missed a spanking."

But years later, my mother told me the truth.

My father had whispered to her, "Don't wake them. They're safe. That's all that matters."

He had been so scared of losing us. Scared of what could have been. And he masked it with fury because that's what strong fathers sometimes do.

That day, I learned something about love—real love. It doesn't always speak gently. It doesn't always show itself in hugs or praise. Sometimes, it shouts, it panics, it scolds... but only because it cares so deeply.

My father didn't scold me that night. He didn't need to. His fear said it all.

And once again, the orange van had been part of it—racing through the storm, carrying a father's heart that would rather drown than lose one of his children.

The First Kiss

Her name was Ilona.

Even now, decades later, I can't remember her face clearly, but I remember the way she made me feel. She was one of those girls with light hair and even lighter laughter, the kind that seemed to float in the air like dandelion seeds. Every time she came near, I felt a flutter in my chest, a rush of something I didn't yet have words for. It was innocent, pure, the soft stirring of boyhood emotion. But to me, it felt enormous.

We were both nine. Childhood friends, schoolmates, maybe something more in the way children feel things before they can name them. There wasn't much to it, just little glances, walking close to each other on the way home from school, sitting near each other at the park, and sharing snacks in awkward silence. But I carried butterflies in my stomach every time I thought of her. And one day, without warning, it happened.

She kissed me.

We were in the schoolyard, near the swing sets. No one was around. She looked at me, leaned forward quickly, and kissed me on the cheek. Just one soft, fleeting moment. But it was enough to stop time.

I stood there frozen, heart pounding, cheeks burning, unsure if I should run or stay forever. She laughed—just a little—and skipped away. And I floated home like I was in a dream.

For days, I couldn't stop smiling. I walked with a new bounce in my step, like I had been let in on some beautiful secret of the world. I didn't tell anyone. I didn't need to. It was mine, that memory—a private joy. A seed of love planted in the soft earth of my boyhood.

Looking back now, that kiss was more than just a first. It was the last pure moment of childhood before everything began to change. Before illness. Before sadness. Before I had to grow up far too soon.

That single kiss, sweet and simple, became a symbol of everything I would soon have to leave behind. It was my last taste of innocence.

The Last Goodbye

Not long after Ilona's kiss, I began to sense a change in the world around me.

It started with small things. The light in our house felt dimmer, even when the sun was out. My mother didn't smile as easily anymore. My father moved slower as if the weight of something invisible was pressing on his shoulders. He still kissed us every morning, tried to play, and cracked quiet jokes, but behind his eyes, something was different. Something heavy.

The weekend trips to the farmers' market stopped. No more waking up before dawn to load the van with vegetables. No more pastries in the evening runs to the concert venues—no more laughter echoing from the front seat of the orange van. My father had stopped going to work. He was home every day, sitting in his favorite chair, quietly watching us play from a distance instead of joining in.

He looked thinner. He barely ate. And my mother... she stopped cooking full meals. She stopped humming in the kitchen. I'd catch her staring at the wall or wiping her eyes with her apron when she thought no one was watching. At night, I heard her crying.

Then, one day, I came home from school, and my father wasn't there.

"He's in the hospital for a few days," my mother said, trying to sound normal. But her voice cracked. Her hands shook. And her eyes betrayed a truth I didn't yet understand.

The house changed after that. It was quiet—too quiet. My grandmother came from Turkey to stay with us. My mother disappeared to the hospital for long stretches. We weren't allowed to visit him. I didn't know why. I was just a boy waiting for his father to come back and bring the laughter with him.

And then, one afternoon, it happened.

The orange van. Our orange van. The one that had carried my childhood. The one that took us across Europe and back. The one where we ate sandwiches and sang Turkish songs. The one my father drove like a captain steering a ship of dreams...

It was sold.

I watched from the window as two strangers came to take it. I screamed. I kicked. I tried to open the front door, but my uncles held me back. "Don't let them take it!" I shouted, thrashing in their arms. "It's ours! It's my father's! Tell him to stop them!"

But he wasn't there to stop them. He wasn't there at all.

I stood on the pavement, helpless, watching it drive away. That bright orange van—the vessel of everything I loved—disappeared into the misty street. And something inside me collapsed. I screamed until I had no breath. I wept until my legs gave out.

That night, we were told the truth.

The doctors had given my father six months to live.

He was still conscious, still able to speak, and he used what strength he had to ask my mother for two final promises:

That she would take him home to his village in Turkey so he could die where he was born…

And that she would return with us—his children—to her family's village to raise us with the support he could no longer provide.

He wanted us to be safe. He didn't want her to be alone. He knew what was coming.

She promised him.

Within weeks, everything was packed. Friends stopped by to say goodbye. There were no jokes. No parties. Only heavy silences and the quiet ache of goodbyes that came too soon.

My father was flown ahead to a hospital near my mother's village. And we—my mother, my siblings, and I—boarded a one-way flight, carrying only what we needed.

The cobblestone streets of Hengelo faded behind us. The house on Elisabeth Street. The creek across the road. The garden where I built my clay house. The smell of my mother's cooking. The laughter of my sisters. The dreams of my father. All left behind.

The boy who once floated home from a first kiss was now walking away from everything he'd ever known.

And that's how my childhood ended.

Not with a graduation, or a final school bell, or even a goodbye hug…

But with sorrow.

With silence.

With the memory of a van driving away and a father who never did come home.

CHAPTER TWO

The Village and Beyond

The Journey to the Village

The orange van was gone.

Sold quietly, like everything else we couldn't carry with us. My father had insisted. "We won't need it where we're going," he had said just before being flown ahead to Turkey alone to be admitted into a hospital near his hometown. He was too weak to stay in Hengelo, too sick to hide it anymore. That van—the beating heart of every road trip, every carnival, every drop of joy from my childhood—was just… gone.

I was nine years old.

Our youngest sibling, just a year old, was cradled in my mother's arms as she tried to navigate the chaos of the airport. Her other arm dragged a rolling suitcase while her eyes scanned the signs overhead, trying to hide the fear swelling beneath the surface. My older sisters flanked her, silent and alert. My younger brother clung to my hand. And I, still a child myself, tried to act like a little man — watching, guarding, and understanding more than anyone thought I did.

We had one-way tickets to Istanbul. Nothing else. No van. No return.

Schiphol Airport was crowded, but we moved through it like a slow, grieving cloud. My mother juggled a crying baby, passports, bags, and four young children. The stroller kept folding in on itself.

My brother kept asking where Baba was. I kept telling him, "We'll see him soon," though I wasn't sure anymore.

The flight was a blur. I sat by the window, looking out at a world slipping away beneath us. My sisters took turns holding the baby, my mother whispering prayers under her breath as if the plane were being held aloft by them alone. I kept trying to remember how my father smelled — a mix of cologne, sweat, and tomatoes from the market — but the memory was already starting to fade.

When we landed in Istanbul, it was humid and loud. The terminal buzzed with unfamiliar energy. A few minutes after we stepped outside, I saw a familiar figure weaving through the crowd: my mother's brother, our uncle. He had driven hours to come get us.

He hugged my mother without words. Just a long, tight embrace. Then he patted my head, helped with the bags, and ushered us into his dusty car. There was no booster seat for the baby, no snacks or music, just the soft rattling of tools in the trunk and the kind of silence that only families facing grief can carry together.

The ride to the village was long. We passed dry hills, cracked roads, old men sitting on crates, and shepherds herding their flocks through dusty fields. I watched everything from the window, searching for anything that reminded me of the Netherlands. There was nothing. Not a single familiar shape or sound. Even the sun felt closer, harsher.

And yet, I had been here before.

Every summer, our orange van would rumble down this same dusty road, windows open, Turkish music playing, my father behind the wheel with a grin on his face. We'd arrive to hugs and laughter, sleep on the same floor mats, chase chickens in the yard, and then, after a few days, head to my father's village to see the rest of the family. It was part of our grand annual road trip—a loop of joy, reunions, Turkish tea, and roadside watermelon.

But this time, everything was different.

The van was gone.

My father wasn't with us.

And we hadn't come to visit us. We had come to stay.

As we stepped into my grandparent's home, the house we used to run through barefoot and giggling, everything felt unfamiliar. The walls were the same. The rugs hadn't moved. Even the scent of tea and wood smoke lingered just as I remembered, but the magic was gone.

This time, we weren't guests. We were refugees from our own life.

The house was small, with thick stone walls and a sagging roof of sun-dried tiles. Smoke rose faintly from the chimney. A cracked wooden door opened to a simple, two-room layout. My grandfather was gone. My grandmother greeted us at the door, wiping her hands on her apron, her face already wet with tears. She took the baby from my mother's arms and began to weep softly.

We had arrived.

That night, my mother barely had time to unpack. We received news that my father's condition had worsened. He had been transferred to a larger hospital. Without hesitation, she packed a small bag and left before dawn to be by his side. She kissed each of us one by one—my sisters, my brother, and the baby. When she came to me, she paused, cupped my cheek, and held my gaze just a moment longer.

"Take care of them until I come back," she said.

And then she walked out into the night, leaving us in a house we had only ever known as visitors, now alone in it.

That night, I lay beside my siblings on thin mats laid out on the rug-covered floor. The air smelled of ash and sheep wool. A single lantern flickered in the corner. My grandmother hummed quietly while rocking the baby. My sisters whispered to each other in the dark. And I stared at the ceiling, listening to the sound of crickets and the thudding of my own heart.

I was nine years old, and everything I'd ever known had disappeared.

The Village Life

The village had always been a stop on our summer road trips. After a few days of dirt roads, fresh eggs, and sleeping under mosquito nets, we moved on to the next family visit. But this time, there was no next stop. No van waiting to take us back to Holland. This time, we were not visitors.

This time, we were villagers.

My mother's family home was already full before we arrived — two bedrooms shared between three generations. My grandfather and grandmother lived there year-round. My older uncle, married with three kids around our age, lived in one room with his family. My younger uncle, single, came and went from a gas station my father had built about an hour away, closer to the town of Sarıkaya. And now, suddenly, five more children and our mother — who would soon leave again to be with my father at the hospital — had been folded into this crowded, crumbling house.

There were guard dogs outside — massive Kangal shepherds, not pets, but protectors. They barked at everything. At night, they roamed the perimeter, eyes glowing in the dark. The cats weren't pets either; they earned their place chasing the rats that scurried along the stone walls. Behind the house, in a small barn connected to the kitchen by a narrow corridor, lived a restless cluster of animals: chickens, a few cows, sheep, and a donkey. At night, I would lie awake and hear them rustling, snorting, shifting in the dark — a constant reminder that life here never truly went silent.

Every morning, just after sunrise, my grandfather would rise, grab his sickle and cloth bag, and call for me to follow him. He walked slowly, dragging one foot slightly behind the other, a limp from an old injury, but he never once let it slow him down. We would trek together for half an hour to his land, about five acres of golden wheat fields stretching beneath the open sky.

The tools he used were ancient with wooden handles, iron blades, and hand-woven rope for binding the cut wheat into bundles. We would cut until our arms burned. I was nine, and every part of me ached from trying to keep up. By midday, just when I thought I would collapse, my grandmother would appear with lunch: cold spring water, bread, cheese, olives, and tomatoes from the garden. We'd sit on a cloth beneath the shade of a tree, eat in silence, and then go back to cutting. It felt endless. And I hated every second of it.

I wasn't made for this life. Or at least, I believed I wasn't.

Back home, in the Netherlands, I rode my bike to school. I had friends. Toys. Electricity. Clean clothes. Here, everything smelled of smoke, sweat, and soil. The toilet was an outhouse; the water had to be carried in buckets, and nothing ever truly felt clean. My sisters helped my grandmother, spending the days collecting eggs, milking the cows, and weeding the garden. My uncle's wife baked bread nearly every day in the outdoor stone oven, stacking it in baskets to store for winter. They all seemed to belong to this rhythm. I did not.

My older uncle tended to the animals and the herds. He'd take the cows to graze and lead the sheep into the mountains, sometimes staying overnight with nothing but a shotgun and one of the fierce Kangal dogs for protection. He'd occasionally take me along. We would climb for hours, the sheep clattering along narrow paths. At night, we'd set up camp under the stars. There were no tents, just a blanket, a fire, and the fear of wolves. We took turns staying awake. If the dogs barked or we saw glowing eyes, we'd yell, scream, throw rocks, and, if needed, fire a shot into the air.

I was terrified. I didn't show it, but inside I was unraveling.

This wasn't my life.

This wasn't me.

I didn't know how to become this version of myself — a boy who feared wolves, cut wheat with his bare hands and waited days for word of his father. There were no phones in the village—no way to call the hospital. News traveled only with people coming and going between Sarıkaya and the village, and even then, no one ever had anything concrete to share. Days passed. Then more. And more. Every night, I came home hoping someone would say something — anything — about Baba. And every night, there was only silence.

The hotel my father had built in Sarıkaya stood empty. He had dreamed big, and he saw the potential in that small municipality of 3,000 people nestled among Roman ruins and natural hot springs. The town was ancient and full of untapped promise like a diamond still buried in dirt. That's why he built the gas station. That's why he poured every lira into that hotel. He saw a future.

And now he was fading in some hospital bed while his son tried to learn how to fight off wolves and carry bundles of wheat bigger than his own body.

I didn't cry. Not then. I think part of me had gone numb.

But deep down, I was angry.

Angry at life. Angry at the village. Angry that my father had vanished into silence. And mostly angry that everyone else seemed to be adjusting, while I was still lost.

The Wolves and the Tree

Then came the day my uncle took me herding into the mountains.

We left at sunrise with around forty sheep and walked for nearly three hours, climbing slowly as the landscape shifted from dry fields to rocky hills. The sheep moved like a wave of wool and dust, and my uncle carried a shotgun slung across his back. We reached a wide grazing spot high above the village, and while the animals spread out to feed, I sat on a rock, already exhausted. My body wasn't made for this. My lungs hurt. My legs ached. I felt dizzy.

"I want to go back," I told him. "I'll find my way. I remember the path."

He looked at me for a long moment, serious and doubtful. "Are you sure?"

I nodded. I was trying to be brave or maybe just trying to escape the isolation, the hunger, the heat, and the sound of animals that never stopped.

He gave me a piece of bread, pointed toward the path we'd taken, and watched as I started the journey home.

At first, I felt confident. I followed the same trail we had come up on. The sun was still above the mountains. I told myself I'd be home before it set. But after two hours of walking, I still couldn't see the village. No rooftops. No people. No smoke from the chimneys. Just more mountain. More trees. And now the light was starting to change.

The panic crept in slowly, like a shadow.

No one knew I was missing. My uncle thought I'd be home by now. My grandfather thought I was still with my uncle. There were no phones. No way to call for help. I was a nine-year-old boy in the Turkish wilderness, alone, with nothing but a few crumbs of bread in my pocket.

The sky dimmed.

The wind picked up.

And then I heard it — a long, echoing howl.

Wolves.

I froze. My heart pounded so loudly I could hear it in my ears. I turned to run—not back to my uncle because I didn't have the strength or the time. I ran forward blindly, hoping the village would appear around the next bend. But it didn't. Just more trees. And the howls… they were closer now. Sharper. There were many of them.

Then I saw a large tree, rising above the brush like a pillar of hope. I sprinted toward it, reaching out for the lowest branch. As I climbed, my mind flashed back to a memory from behind our house in Hengelo, where my cousins and I had once climbed a tree and gotten in trouble. My father had been so angry. That memory—sweet, ordinary, safe—hit me like a wave.

I pulled myself higher, bark scratching my arms, breath short and sharp. I reached the top and looked down.

They were there.

A pack of wolves circled the base of the tree, howling and snarling. Their eyes glowed in the dark. My body was shaking. I gripped the branch like it was the only thing keeping me alive — and it was.

And in that moment, suspended above death, I didn't feel brave. I felt small. I wanted to scream for my mother. I wanted my father's arms around me. I wanted to hear him scold me for climbing a tree just so I could hear his voice again.

The fear turned into something deeper: a flood of sadness.

I cried.

I cried hard, quietly, choking on the tears as the wolves kept circling. I was alone, cold, hungry, and broken. My arms were trembling. My legs were going numb. I was sure I wouldn't make it through the night.

And then I heard his voice, not in my ears, but in my heart.

"Don't give up, son. This is not how the day will end."

It was what he used to tell me during long market days. I'd get tired helping him sell vegetables, my feet aching, my spirit low.

He'd look down at me with a gentle but firm smile and say, "Stand strong. The day will pass. We'll rest later. Not now."

So, that's what I did.

I held on.

I pictured him stacking tomatoes, wiping his brow, and nodding at me with pride. I reminded myself that pain is not forever and that morning always comes. I talked to him in my head all night. I repeated his words like a prayer.

By dawn, the wolves were gone.

I stayed in the tree until the sky turned blue and the sounds of birds replaced the howls of the night. When I finally climbed down, my legs gave out beneath me. I staggered. I limped. But I walked. All the way back to the village.

When I appeared at the door, my grandfather's face turned pale. "Where have you been?"

I told him everything. He was furious, not at me, but at my uncle. He wanted to storm off and punish him. But I stopped him.

"This was my choice," I said. "And I learned from it. Don't blame anyone."

And I meant it.

Because that night changed me.

That night, I discovered something I would carry for the rest of my life: I do not need anyone to save me from a situation I created. I will face it. I will endure it. I will survive it.

That tree in the mountains became a symbol for me—a place of terror and rebirth. I climbed it as a lost child. I came down from it with the mindset of a man.

And that mindset would one day carry me across an ocean, build businesses, employ people, raise a family, and make something beautiful out of pain.

That night with the wolves didn't destroy me.

It built me.

My Father's Final Days

It happened just a few days after the night I had spent in a tree, surrounded by wolves, holding on to my life and to my father's memory like it was a rope keeping me from falling apart.

We had just finished working the land, my grandfather and I. My arms were sore, my face caked with dust and sun. We were walking the familiar dirt road back toward the house. I saw the old, rusty car that belonged to my uncle, parked outside before he did. My grandmother and uncle were helping my siblings get into it.

A cold wave of dread washed over me.

I knew.

The moment I had pushed from my mind—the moment I still clung to hope would never come—had arrived. Something inside me cracked. My knees weakened. My body kept moving forward, but my soul wanted to run the other way. I would rather keep hoping than know for certain. I would rather not know than live in a world without him.

I stopped walking.

My grandfather, a few paces ahead, noticed the stillness. He turned around. But before he looked at me, he locked eyes with my grandmother and my uncle — and in that single glance, he understood.

There were tears on my grandmother's face.

My grandfather came back to me and knelt in the dirt. He placed a firm, warm hand on my shoulder. His eyes were tired, but his voice was soft.

"I want you to be strong for your siblings," he said.

And that's when the first tear broke loose—hot, quiet, sliding down my cheek. He gently wiped it away and pulled me into him. I collapsed into his arms and let out a scream so deep that it felt like it came from the center of the earth. My sisters heard it. They rushed out of the car, sobbing, running toward me. We all folded into each other, a pile of pain, children crushed beneath the weight of a moment no child should ever have to bear.

Even the adults couldn't hold back their tears. It was too much. Five innocent kids, losing the man who had loved them, taught them, shielded them. Watching us cry like that shattered something in them, too.

My uncle gently gathered us.

"We don't have much time," he said softly. "The hospital discharged him. He's at the apart hotel… your mother asked me to get you. He's still breathing, but it won't be long."

The ride to Sarıkaya took about forty-five minutes. But it felt like an eternity.

None of us spoke in full sentences; we just cried. We held each other, took turns holding our baby brother, and kissed his forehead again and again. It was the only thing we could control, to love one another as hard as we could on that ride because we knew what was waiting.

When we arrived, there was a crowd gathered at the hotel entrance — people I didn't recognize, distant relatives, neighbors, and loved ones who had come to see my father one last time. As we approached, they stepped aside, parting like a sea of grief to let us pass.

We climbed the stairs to the second floor. And that's when I heard it.

"Agıt."

The mournful songs of Turkish women — sung through tears, voices trembling, rising and falling in rhythm with heartbreak. I could hear my mother's voice among them, louder than the rest. Singing, crying, telling his life story through the agony of farewell.

She sang of how they met, how they married, how they left this village for a foreign land. How they built a beautiful family, how he fell ill, how she was now left alone—and how she prayed for his soul to be welcomed in the afterlife.

We were all sobbing before we even entered the room.

But nothing could have prepared me for what I saw when I did.

In the center of the room, lying still under a thin white sheet, was my father. The man I adored, my hero, the strong, broad-shouldered man who once lifted crates of vegetables like they were feathers. The man who drove us across Europe in the orange van. The man who taught me how to stand tall in the market.

That man… was gone. Or nearly gone.

He had lost all his hair. His face was gaunt, hollow, unrecognizable. His mouth hung open. His eyes stared straight into nothing, no movement, no light. It's just the abyss.

He was still breathing, barely—a soft, uneven sound like a candle flickering.

I stepped closer, desperate to lock eyes with him, to say something — anything — that might reach the part of him still holding on. But his gaze didn't meet mine. It floated above me as if he were already halfway gone.

And then, his body arched slightly.

A loud, painful breath escaped his mouth.

The room fell silent, then erupted with cries. The women sang louder. My mother screamed his name. My sister fainted. The pain was unbearable — a sound you don't hear but feel.

Then came the second breath.

Louder. Slower. Heavier. His chest lifted. His mouth trembled. And then fell again.

A hush swept the room. Everyone leaned in.

And then, the final breath.

It was the longest. The loudest. The most human. It rose like thunder, held for a moment… and then fell into a whisper. A tiny sound. Fading. Fading…

Gone.

Just like that.

A stillness fell that no one dared break. And in that silence, I understood something I never had before.

The world does not stop when your heart breaks. It just moves on without you.

City of Ankara – New School and Farmers Market

August 1st, 1986, in the quiet heat of the afternoon, my father took his last breath. He was just 39 years old, a man full of dreams, strength, and love. Our father. Our leader. The patriarch of our family.

In the days that followed, people came from villages, cities, and distant corners of the country to say goodbye. His funeral was held in Sarıkaya, near the apart hotel he had built and the gas station he had started with his own hands. He had chosen that place with purpose, believing in its future, in the healing waters that bubbled from ancient Roman ruins. And now, it would be the place where we buried him.

I remember sitting beside his grave long after the last prayer had been said, long after the others began drifting away. I was exhausted, not just from the funeral, but from everything. From the sickness, the silence, the heartbreak, the wolves, the fear, the unknown. My body was there, but my heart had stopped months earlier. I didn't want to leave him. How could we walk away and just... go on?

But eventually, we did.

We returned to the village, and the mourning continued. In our culture, grief stretches for forty days — forty days of sadness, of visitors, of soft voices and headscarves soaked with tears. For us, it would never really end.

But life, in its cruel indifference, kept moving.

There was no school in the village, only dust and chores and echoes of the past. My grandfather and mother decided it was time for us to leave. We needed a future and the village couldn't give us one. Ankara, the capital, would be our second chance.

My great-uncle lived there. With the money my father had saved—enough for a small three-bedroom apartment—we packed what little we had, left the sheep and the fields behind, and made the journey to a city that felt like another country.

I was still broken. Still angry. I watched people around me begin to smile again, joke, and live. But I couldn't. I felt like even smiling was a betrayal of my father's memory. I resented everyone for moving on. I didn't want the pain to end because the pain meant he was still with me.

As we entered Ankara, I stared out the window at the endless buildings, shops, and apartment blocks. The city was alive with people, horns, and movement. On a hill in the middle of it all, Ankara Castle sat like a silent guardian, watching the chaos unfold beneath it. There was something ancient in that stone, something I didn't yet understand, but it made me feel like maybe, just maybe, we were part of something bigger.

For the first few nights, we stayed with my great-uncle while preparing our own apartment. Relatives brought beds, chairs, a table, and a couch — not much, but enough. My grandmother, my father's mother, moved in with us to support my mother. She had no money, and my mother had no income. Because my father had worked in the Netherlands but died before retirement, we wouldn't receive his full pension, just a small monthly payment, barely enough for food.

Still, we made it work.

Within days, all four of us were enrolled in school. It was a 30-minute walk each way, through unfamiliar neighborhoods and suspicious eyes. The school was nothing like the clean, bright schools of the Netherlands. The building looked like a prison, with iron gates and thick walls. There was no gym, no playground, no swimming pool. The classrooms were overcrowded with about 80 to 100 kids per room, squeezed shoulder-to-shoulder, four to a desk.

We all wore black uniforms with white neck collars, like little soldiers. I was placed in third grade. I had never attended school in Turkey before. I spoke Turkish with an accent. I knew nothing about the country's history or customs. The first few days were a blur of confusion and whispers.

The bullying came fast.

Kids sensed we were different, that we didn't belong and that we had no father. No older brother to defend us. They called us "foreign pigs." They mocked our accent. They pushed us, laughed at our clothes, and made us feel like trash. Every neighborhood had its gang of kids, and they protected each other, but no one protected us.

I tried to keep my head down. My sisters did the same. We walked in silence, hoping to make it to school without being noticed. But hope doesn't protect you from fists or words.

At the same time, I knew we needed money.

One weekend, while walking through a local farmers' market, I remembered something my father once told me. It wasn't just about selling vegetables. "You can sell anything," he had said. "The work isn't what you sell. The work is standing tall and learning how to sell." He had once pointed out an old man at a market in Germany selling ice-cold water from a wheelbarrow. "That man will sell out before anyone else," my father said.

I couldn't sell produce. I had nothing to sell.

But I could sell water.

I found two large containers, filled them halfway, and froze them overnight. By morning, I topped them with cold water. I borrowed a copper cup from home, and with both containers—heavy as bricks—I carried them across two neighborhoods to the market.

It was backbreaking. My arms were numb. I stopped ten times on the way.

But when I got there, I found a quiet corner near the exit and waited.

Soon, an old woman approached. She asked for a drink but said she had no money.

And at that moment, I remembered another lesson from my father about the German homeless man who came to our market stall in Europe. I had watched my father slice a tomato and cucumber, salt them, serve them with respect, and place his right hand on his heart as he nodded to the man.

"Sometimes," my father had said, "you give to the universe… and it gives back tenfold."

So, I gave the woman the water. I stood tall. I placed my hand on my chest and nodded respectfully, and she smiled as if she had been handed gold.

Within an hour, I sold out.

I ran home with more joy than I had felt in months. I bought candies, cakes, and even small gifts for my siblings and grandmother. I handed the rest to my mother.

I expected her to cry, to praise me, to hug me the way she used to when Baba was still alive.

She didn't.

She smiled gently and said, "Next time, don't waste money on candy. We need to save it for rainy days."

That was it.

But it was enough.

Because in that moment, I knew two things:

> I could take care of us.

> My father was still teaching me — even from the grave.

The Rage and the Birth of a Fighter

The next weekend couldn't come fast enough.

I had a plan. This time, I filled four large water containers. I would take only two to the bazaar and leave the others in the freezer. As soon as I sold out, I'd run home, swap them, refill the empty ones with fresh water, and repeat. I had learned the hustle. I was growing smarter. And for the first time since my father fell ill in Hengelo, I felt… alive.

I walked into the market like I belonged.

This time, I wasn't just offering water; I was selling. Just like I used to with my father at the market. I raised my voice with pride, shouting across the lanes:

"The coldest water in the bazaar! The cheapest water in the bazaar!"

Sometimes I'd shout: "Buy two, get one free!" I switched between slogans to keep people interested, just like Baba used to.

And it worked. I was busy. My spot was packed.

Here and there, someone would ask for water and quietly admit they had no money. That's when I'd place my right hand on my heart, nod, and serve them with honor. Just like my father had taught me — give to the universe, and it will give back tenfold.

As I worked, I often looked up at the sky.

"Can you see me, Baba?" I'd wonder. But I always answered myself the same way:

"You're not up there. You're in here."

And I'd place my hand on my chest.

He was with me. In my heart. In my head. In every move I made.

That weekend, I sold out again. Twice.

I turned the money over to my mother — no praise, no hugs, just a soft smile, and the reminder:

"Don't waste it on candy this time. We must save for rainy days."

I didn't care. My reward wasn't her approval. It was the feeling inside me, knowing I was carrying my family forward, even if no one said it aloud.

But during the week, the war continued.

The bullying never stopped. If anything, it grew worse. The walks to school were like crossing enemy lines. Every neighborhood had gangs of kids who protected their own, and we weren't one of them. We were still the foreign pigs. I hated every step of those walks. I kept my head down. My sisters did too.

But I had found something that gave me light: the weekends, the water, the market.

Still, the pain, the sadness, the rage — it never really left. It waited, just below the surface.

Then, one night, it happened.

I woke up from a nightmare, drenched in sweat, struggling to catch my breath. As I sat up in bed, trying to calm myself, I saw him — an old man with long white hair and a white beard dressed in glowing white robes, sitting at the edge of my bed.

I screamed. My mother rushed in, panic in her eyes, but I couldn't stop pointing.

"He's right there! Don't you see him?"

She saw nothing.

But I saw him clearly. And strangely… he was smiling.

His face was gentle and peaceful, and as his eyes met mine, I felt an overwhelming warmth fill my chest. The fear faded. The screaming stopped. Everything around me went quiet like I was floating in a trance.

My mother was still there, shaking me, yelling my name, but her voice sounded distant, muffled like she was underwater.

And then he spoke.

"My dear," he said in the softest, most calming voice I've ever heard, "you will be fine."

And just like that, he was gone.

Vanished like a cloud.

My body relaxed. My eyes closed. And I fell into a deeper sleep than I'd known in months.

The next morning, I felt different. Stronger. Calmer. Certain. Something had shifted. Whether it was an angel, a dream, or a visit from beyond, it didn't matter. I believed it. And that belief gave me power.

That weekend, I went back to the market, but this time, I brought my little brother with me.

He would help. Together, we'd sell more. We worked the market just like before, yelling slogans, giving water, respecting the elders, smiling with pride. We sold out fast. People loved us.

Then, as we were getting ready to close our stand, I saw them.

A group of older boys swaggering toward us with hard faces. I knew instantly—this was trouble.

They were just a few years older but bigger and stronger, and they had no intention of buying water.

They came straight to our stand, knocked over the containers, shattered them, and spilled everything.

Then one of them leaned in closely and said:

"This is our turf. If we see you again, you'll leave in pieces."

I stared at the ruins of my stand.

All that work. The early mornings. The weight. The freezing. The money for my family. Gone.

I didn't look at them.

I didn't speak.

I just felt something start to boil in my chest.

Rage.

Not just from that moment — but from all of it.

The bullying. The name-calling. The beatings.

The day my father told us he was sick.

The night he left.

The dirt over his grave.

All of it.

I snapped.

I attacked.

No thinking. No fear. Just fists. I hit one and kicked another. Someone punched me in the side, but I didn't feel it. I kept swinging. My little brother screamed. Adults ran in. People tried to pull me off.

But I was screaming over and over:

"You will NEVER touch us again! NEVER!"

They ran. Every last one of them.

I stood there, chest heaving, fists bruised, soaked in sweat.

My brother cried.

I hugged him.

Strangers helped us gather what was left of our stand. I told my brother not to tell anyone what happened. I didn't want any pity.

But inside, I felt something I hadn't felt in a long time:

Pride.

Not for the fight. But for standing my ground. For protecting my brother. For refusing to let the world walk all over me.

The next morning, everything changed.

On our walk to school, the usual bullies looked down. Said nothing.

At school, kids whispered.

A few classmates ran up to me.

"Everyone's talking about it," they said.

"They're scared of you."

And for the first time, they weren't laughing at us.

They left us alone.

My siblings walked freely. Heads high.

I had become something I never intended to be—a protector, a fighter, a leader. Without meaning to, I had my own little "gang" now; boys who followed me stood with me. I wasn't a foreign pig anymore. I was Api. And no one messed with Api.

The fights didn't stop—word spread. New gangs from other neighborhoods came looking for me.

But I was ready.

I kept working in the market, selling water, and bringing in money for my family. And now, I wasn't just helping them survive; I was keeping them safe.

That life—the rage, the honor, the brotherhood—carried me all the way through the end of 8th grade.

I was about to start high school.

But I had no idea that the summer ahead would change everything again.

The Day I Stood Alone

Every summer, without fail, as soon as the school year ended, my mother would pack our bags and ship us off to her village. It wasn't a question. It was tradition. My siblings and I would board the bus to that dusty little place nestled in the dry heart of Anatolia, far from the chaos of Ankara. For them, it was summer. For me, it was a sentence.

I didn't hate the village. I hated what it did to me.

I'd spend endless days working my grandfather's land, dragging heavy tools through cracked earth under a sun that showed no mercy. Some days, I was with my older uncle, tending to sheep and goats. Other days, I was at my father's gas station, the one my younger uncle managed after my father passed. He barely made enough to support himself, but he held onto it like it was a shrine to the man we both lost too soon. I wasn't paid for the work. I wasn't thanked. It was expected because I was a strong boy and my father was gone.

But the summer after middle school, I did the unthinkable.

I said no.

I told my mother I wasn't going. I told her I was staying in Ankara.

She stared at me as if I had cursed. My grandfather and my uncles were furious. To them, I was already a problem child. They didn't see the boy who defended his siblings, who stood his ground in a world that treated him like an outsider. They saw a stubborn, angry kid who refused to fall in line. I had never once started a fight, but I never backed down from one, either. I was living in a war zone, and I fought to survive it.

I never came home and complained. I never made excuses. I worked, I studied, I bled, quietly. But it didn't matter. The neighbors whispered. "He's a thug," they said. "Our kids are scared of him." I never stole a dime. Never hurt anyone who didn't bring it on themselves. But the label stuck.

So, when I refused to go to the village, they made their decision.

They gave me two options.

Go to the village. Or go to a boarding facility for troubled kids in another part of Ankara.

I chose the facility without hesitation.

Not because I feared the village; I just knew I needed to break the cycle. I had no more fear left in me. The version of life I once knew—safe, steady, full of love—had vanished years ago. This was survival now. If I had to be alone to grow, then so be it.

A few days later, I was dropped off at the facility by one of my uncles. I carried a plastic bag with a few shirts and no money in my pocket. Everything I needed—food, bed, shelter—would be provided. It felt like both an ending and a beginning. My uncle patted my shoulder and said, "I'll be back in three months to pick you up for high school."

But none of us knew that would be the last time I ever lived under the same roof with my family.

As we walked through the iron gates, I saw other kids arriving. Some cried, clutching their parents, begging not to be left behind. Others looked around, wide-eyed and frightened. Me? I felt strangely calm. I wasn't scared. I wasn't even sad. I was… curious. Curious about who I'd meet. Curious about who I might become.

The facility had five floors, each one holding thirty rooms packed with four bunk beds. The first floor had a cafeteria that served three meals a day. The second had classrooms and a prayer room. Tall metal fences surrounded the property, with a heavy iron gate that opened at 9 a.m. and locked shut by 8 p.m. If you attended the morning classes and evening prayers, you were free to leave during the day. Break the rules, and you were out, no second chances.

To some kids, this felt like a prison. To me, it felt like freedom.

Sure, I was giving up my side hustle—the water stand I ran in the bazaars. There was no fridge here and no market nearby. But what

I was gaining was bigger: distance from judgmental eyes, from the whispers, from the tired routine that kept me trapped.

This wasn't punishment.

This was a possibility.

Within days of arriving, I knew what I had to do.

In a place like this, weakness was a scent and boys who smelled of it were devoured quickly. So, I asserted myself. I wasn't loud or reckless, but I made it clear: no one would step on me. I wasn't here to be bullied or disrespected. But I also wasn't here to be feared. I wanted something more valuable than fear: respect.

I started building quiet relationships with the adults in charge — the ones who monitored the halls, who handed out the passes to leave the grounds, who decided if you belonged. I wanted them to see me not as the kid they probably read about in a report but as someone disciplined, someone who followed the rules, someone they could trust. If I earned their trust, I earned my freedom, at least during the day.

Every morning in the cafeteria, a stack of fresh newspapers would arrive, folded neatly on the corner table near the milk station. Most kids ignored them. I didn't. I began flipping straight to the back, to the section where the job listings lived. This was how many kids found work—stocking shelves at corner stores, sweeping floors in mechanic shops, packing boxes at factories nearby. It was hard work, but it gave them coins in their pockets and something to do beyond these walls.

But none of it interested me.

I wasn't just looking for a job.

I was looking for a door.

For days, I read those listings, circling and crossing out one after another. Grocery stocker? No. Assembly line assistant? No. I didn't know what I was looking for, only that I'd know it when I saw it.

Then, one day, it appeared.

A new listing, printed in bold black letters, tucked between ads for delivery drivers and warehouse helpers. It was different. The job itself didn't sound glamorous, not at first glance, but something about it pulled me in. It was like the words glowed off the page. I felt it in my chest: this was it.

What I didn't know was that this small newspaper ad—barely a paragraph long—would unlock a completely different world. A world of speed, risk, secrets, and motion. A world that would change the trajectory of my life, put me face-to-face with powerful men, and eventually lead me far beyond the gates of that iron-fenced facility.

It wasn't just a job.

It was the beginning of an entirely different life.

The ad was small. Just a few lines wedged between warehouse postings and apprentice gigs.

"Looking for a male model between the ages of 12 to 16 for an upcoming fashion show."

Open auditions. No experience is necessary. Address and date listed below.

That was it. No company name. No phone number. Just an invitation. But to me, it might as well have been written in gold ink. I read it again. And again. Something about those words stirred a strange mix of emotions in me — curiosity, excitement, and a feeling I hadn't felt in a long time: hope.

It was a week away. The location was about an hour's walk from the facility, not too far, but not a direction I was allowed to go.

Because here was the catch.

To get out, even for a few hours, you needed permission. And permission came with rules.

You had to present where you were going and what you were doing, and in most cases, it had to be a pre-approved job or religious activity. This place, despite its cafeteria and metal gates, was built on rules, routines, and a moral compass tightly wound by religious doctrine. Fashion? Modeling? That wasn't just unapproved—it was unheard of.

So, I made a move.

I found another listing. A boring one. Something about warehouse labor, no specific name or address, just vague enough to pass inspection. I wrote that down and submitted my request for a one-day work permit.

The adults reviewed it, nodded, and handed me my pass.

They had no idea I was chasing something else.

Something that had nothing to do with moving boxes.

That day, I folded the newspaper clipping and tucked it into my pocket like it was a ticket to another world. When the iron gates opened that morning, I stepped out—not as a warehouse worker, not even as a troubled kid trying to prove himself. I walked out with a lie in my pocket and a dream in my chest.

This wasn't just about modeling.

This was about the agency. About choosing something for myself—not handed to me, not forced on me, not dictated by fear or survival. It was the first time in a long time that I felt like I was chasing something that was mine.

I didn't know what I'd find at the other end of that walk.

But I knew one thing:

I was no longer just surviving.

I was seeking.

The building was bright and modern — a different world from the one I had just walked out of. As I approached, I saw them: a sea of kids, maybe a hundred or more, dressed like they were headed to a gala. Crisp collars, styled hair, polished shoes. Some looked like they'd just stepped out of fashion magazines.

All of them had someone with them — a parent, an older sibling, maybe even an agent. Everyone… except me.

I stood alone in my worn-out clothes, shoes with tired soles, and a plastic bag tucked under my arm. I must've looked like a kid who wandered in from the wrong part of town. But I didn't feel out of place. I wasn't there to fit in. I was there to stand out.

I got in line.

I have no idea what to expect; there is no script and no backup. Behind the registration desk were closed doors — the mystery on the other side. I gave my name, filled out a quick form, and took a seat near the back of the waiting area. I watched the others, some pacing, others rehearsing. I didn't even know what I was supposed to rehearse.

Then the doors opened.

We were all ushered into a large room with a stage set in the center and seats arranged around it in a semi-circle. The judges — well-dressed, sharp-eyed professionals — took their place at a long table up front.

One of them stood and addressed us.

"This audition is for an upcoming fashion show by a major clothing brand," he said. "We'll be selecting six boys between the ages of 12 and 16. If chosen, you'll receive two weeks of training, and payment will be made after the show."

Then he announced the amount.

My jaw nearly dropped. It was more than I'd make in a month selling cold water under the burning Ankara sun. But that wasn't why my heart started pounding.

It was the opportunity.

The voice inside me whispered: You're not here for the money. You're here to be one of the six.

They explained the audition: one by one, we'd walk the stage. At the end of the runway, we were to stop, face the crowd, and say, "I feel great today because I wore ABC brand clothing today." They didn't reveal the brand name, so "ABC" it was.

Kids began to panic.

Some were practicing their lines aloud, others whispering nervously with their parents coaching them: "Smile more... swing your arms naturally... don't forget the line... say it with energy!" It was chaos... expensive chaos.

Then I saw it. Kids tripping over their own feet. Forgetting the line. Mumbling. Overthinking. Their nerves were louder than their voices.

And then… I remembered something.

A dusty farmers' market in Germany. I was just a little boy. A tomato in one hand. A cucumber in the other. My father's deep, steady voice in my ear:

"Stand in front of the stand.

Yell it loud.

Make them believe it.

Look them in the eye and say —

'Freshest tomatoes! Best cucumbers! Come buy from us!'"

The first time I tried, I was terrified. I stammered, whispered, and avoided eye contact.

He didn't scold me.

He simply said, "Try again. But this time, believe you belong."

Over time, I did.

Whether in Germany or the bazaars of Ankara, I had become a master of grabbing attention, selling something out of nothing. I didn't know it then, but my father wasn't just teaching me how to sell vegetables; he was teaching me how to command a stage.

So, while every other kid had a mother fixing their collar or a father whispering last-minute advice, I had something stronger — memories of a man who once believed in a shy little boy holding vegetables in his tiny hands.

And now I was ready to walk this stage — not as a poor kid from a slum, not as a boy from a religious facility, but as the son of a farmer, the soul of a street vendor, and the voice of a fighter.

I wasn't just going to say the line.

I was going to own it.

Then I heard it.

"Api."

For a moment, the room paused.

All eyes turned toward me. Not because I had done anything unusual but because of my name. "Api" wasn't a name they'd heard before. It didn't exist in the Turkish language. Whispers circled. Parents leaned in. Some kids even chuckled.

But I stood up tall, my shoulders back, my chin high. That name, my name, was not a mistake. It was a legacy. It carried my father's voice, my family's journey, my fight to be seen. I wore it like armor.

I stepped toward the stage with confidence. When I reached the bottom of the stairs, one of the assistants handed me a small slip of paper with the slogan printed on it.

"I feel great today because I wore ABC brand clothing today."

I smiled, shook my head gently, and pushed the paper away.

"No, thank you," I said. "I got this."

And I did.

I took my first step onto the runway and something lit up inside me. It was like I grew wings. Each step thundered with energy. Not arrogance.

Purpose.

I walked with the rhythm of every bazaar I'd ever worked in, every crowd I had once captured selling water under a summer sun. I was no longer the poor kid from the facility. I was a storm in motion.

I reached the edge of the stage.

I stopped.

I gazed into the audience, not just the judges, but all of them. I scanned the faces, eye to eye, just like my father taught me. And with a strong hand gesture, one I improvised from instinct, I projected the line with a voice that filled the entire hall:

"I FEEL GREAT TODAY... BECAUSE I WORE ABC BRAND CLOTHING "

There was no trembling in my voice. No nervous stutter. Just power.

The same power I summoned in the farmers' markets of Germany when my father first placed vegetables in my hands and whispered, "You're not selling tomatoes or cucumbers; you're selling yourself."

And I sold it.

I turned, walked back up the runway, and just before stepping off the stage, I locked eyes with the judges.

And winked.

They smiled.

I returned to my seat, heart pounding but steady. One by one, the others finished. More than an hour passed before the auditions were done, and the room grew quiet as the judges took the stage again.

This was the moment.

They began reading out the names of the six who had been chosen.

One… two… three… four… five…

My name hadn't been called.

I felt my breath catch, but I didn't blink. I held onto that last sliver of hope.

Then, like lightning through a cloud, the final name rang out from the loudspeakers.

"Api."

I exploded from my chair.

Both fists shot into the air as I let out a roar—a full-bodied, uncontrollable victory scream that echoed through the room. I turned to face the audience, fists still raised, shouting like I'd just won a war. Because to me, I had.

This wasn't just an audition.

This was the moment I proved to the world—and to myself—that I was more than the labels, more than the fights, more than the whispers.

I was Api.

And for the first time in years… I felt unstoppable.

The agency put me into an intensive two-week training program.

I absorbed everything: how to walk, how to pause, how to control a room with silence. They taught us posture, facial control, rhythm, and expression. But no one trained like I did. I was hungry. While others tried to memorize steps, I was living the walk, making it mine.

By the end of the two weeks, I knew I wasn't just another boy in the lineup.

I was the show.

The day of the actual fashion show is burned into my memory like fire.

The lights. The music. The crowd.

When I stepped out onto the stage, something in the audience shifted. My presence made people sit forward. The first walk drew gasps—the second — cheers. By the third, the applause rose like a wave. Every time I appeared, the energy lifted.

And the louder they clapped, the stronger I became. Each step fed me. Each cheer filled a space that had been hollow since Hengelo. Since my father. Since the village.

By the end of the show, I wasn't just part of the performance. I was the performance.

I moved the crowd. And they moved me right back.

That moment didn't just win over the crowd, it caught the attention of the agency owner. After the show, he approached me backstage.

"You've got something," he said. "Come back. Twice a week. Let's work."

And that was it. I was in.

I began secretly training twice a week—catwalk skills, facial expressions, postures, choreography, and presence. I learned to breathe on cue, speak with my eyes, and own a room before even stepping into it.

The agency quickly became more than a side gig. I was awarded a small photo shoot, then a local fashion event, then another shoot. Each success fed the next. My name started making rounds in the industry—quietly, discreetly, but surely.

All while I still lived in the dorm.

I kept it all hidden. I followed the rules. Got my day passes. Signed out. Signed in. No one questioned me and I made sure they never had a reason to.

Eventually, I told the agency owner the truth: that I was technically still in a "facility" and had to be careful. He nodded and didn't ask more. He admired my discipline. He kept giving me work.

That summer, I made more money than I had ever seen in my life.

When my siblings returned from the village at the end of the season, I met them at home.

It was the first time we had ever been apart for so long and seeing them again was like exhaling after months of holding my breath. I showered them with gifts, toys, and sweets. I hugged my mother and quietly slipped her an envelope of cash.

"I got a job now," I said. "It's good money."

I didn't tell her what kind of job. I knew she wouldn't understand. But I wanted her to see that I was doing something better, something clean, something dignified. She was proud, I could tell. But also unsettled.

Then I told her the truth.

"I don't want to come back home to live. I want to stay at the dorm during the school year. I'll visit every weekend, I promise. But this… this is better for me."

Her eyes clouded with worry, but she didn't argue. Maybe she saw that I was no longer the boy who needed protection. Maybe she knew she couldn't stop me anyway.

And so, I stayed.

High school began just down the road from the dorm. And somehow, I managed to balance it all:

- Full-time student

- Secret model and event choreographer

- Dorm kid with fake job paperwork

- Weekend son and brother

I became more than just a model. The agency started asking me to train new recruits, choreograph entire shows, sit in coordination meetings, and shadow the planners. I studied how they organized events, managed clients, handled advertising, and controlled backstage chaos. I was learning the entire business from A to Z.

Not from textbooks — from the real world.

By the end of my high school years, I had built something no one could take from me:

- A growing career

- A pocket full of money

- A mind sharpened by real experience

- And grades good enough to silence any critic

I kept my family close. I visited them every weekend. I made sure my siblings felt loved, protected, and proud. I gave my mother what I could and stayed out of the trouble she feared would swallow me.

But I was building something even bigger, a hunger for the next chapter, a taste for more.

The village had taught me to survive.

The dorm had taught me to adapt.

But the stage?

The stage taught me how to shine.

And my next journey was already waiting.

Even as I became someone in the real world — a student, a model, a quiet success story — my nights belonged to someone else.

I couldn't stop dreaming of Hengelo.

It happened often, especially when the dorm was quiet and the lights went out. I'd fall asleep and find myself walking the old path to school, the one that passed the bakery curved past the gardens and ran beside the creek. I'd smell fresh bread. Hear the laughter of my sisters. See the soft grey sky hanging over our little, red-roofed house.

Sometimes, in those dreams, I'd hear the familiar squeak of brakes and there it was: the orange van. Parked right outside. Shining like a warm memory in the mist.

I'd run toward it, yelling, "Baba!" My heart would race with joy.

But just before I could reach it, something would grab me... an invisible force, yanking me back, pulling me far, far away. I'd scream, but no one would hear. I'd wake up drenched in sweat, blinking into the gray walls of the dormitory, breathing like I had just run for my life.

And the pain would hit me all over again.

That I was no longer in Hengelo.

That my father wasn't coming back.

That the van, the house, the garden were all gone.

These dreams didn't disappear over time. They became my shadow.

Even in the middle of my busiest days—planning a fashion show, training a model, acing an exam—the silence would creep in. And in that silence, I'd feel the ache pressing down, begging to be heard.

So, I did what I had learned to do best:

I kept moving.

If I slowed down, the grief caught up.

I filled every hour with something. Work, school, family visits, planning the next event, helping someone with their script, volunteering for backstage prep—anything to avoid falling into that rabbit hole of thoughts that led to a single, unbearable truth:

He was gone.

And I never got to say goodbye.

By the time I reached the end of high school, I was running on sheer momentum. Not because I had a vision. Not because I was chasing a dream.

But because standing still was too painful.

Back then, in Turkey, if you wanted to attend university and attend it for free, you had to pass two national placement exams. They were brutal and competitive and crushed thousands of students each year.

I studied in silence. Alone. No tutors. No fancy prep classes. Just willpower and long nights.

And I passed both of them.

Not just pass. I won a seat at one of the country's most respected programs:

Engineering, at Selçuk University in Konya.

When I got the letter, I didn't feel joy. I felt stillness. Another door had opened but in another new city, with more unknowns. More starting over. More being the stranger.

I broke the news to my family with bittersweet pride. They were happy for me, of course.

Leaving wasn't easy.

The dorm had hardened me. The school had shaped me. But it was the agency that had given me color—made me feel alive, important, full of possibility. For the first time in my life, people saw me, not the immigrant boy, not the village outsider, just Api.

The one who lit up a room. The one who could command a stage. The one who made things happen.

But the day had come. I had passed my exams. I had been accepted into university. A new chapter was calling.

I said goodbye to the people I had worked beside for years — choreographers, designers, models, drivers, coordinators. Some hugged me. Some cried. Others smiled quietly, knowing I wasn't the kind of person who stayed in one place forever.

And then came the agency owner, the man who first saw my fire and kept my secret when I needed it most.

As I shook his hand for the last time, he looked at me and said something that stopped me in my tracks:

"I know one day, your dreams will come true."

I froze. I hadn't told him—or anyone—what my dreams were.

"What dreams?" I asked, half smiling, half confused.

He laughed gently and told me a story. A story he said had quietly passed among the staff, whispered in break rooms and hallways but never spoken to me. They didn't want to discourage me, he said. They didn't want to shatter something delicate.

And then he said it:

"The Parliament cigarette commercial."

Even hearing those words made something stir inside me.

The ad had only run for a few weeks, but I remembered it perfectly.

A long, black stretch limousine parked outside a glowing event hall. Lights pouring from the entrance. A red carpet. A graceful woman in a gown, her arm linked with a man in a black tuxedo. They crossed the street slowly, elegantly, like they owned time itself. And the music, a haunting, cinematic melody that felt like it came from another universe.

Every time the commercial came on the TVs around the agency, I stopped everything to watch it.

I had never told anyone why.

It wasn't the cigarettes. It wasn't even the couple.

It was the feeling. That life. That moment. That presence.

And one day, only once, half-jokingly, I whispered to myself, and maybe to one of the stylists nearby:

"One day, I'll live the same moment that man lived… but mine will be real."

Apparently, they'd heard me. And they believed me more than I believed myself.

At the time, I had no idea where the commercial was shot. I didn't know it was filmed somewhere in America. I didn't even consciously want to leave Turkey yet.

But looking back — that was the first time I reached beyond the walls of my world.

A whisper. A glimpse. A dream that hadn't yet learned how to say its own name.

I left the agency that afternoon with a small envelope of farewell letters, a few warm hugs, and a feeling I couldn't explain.

That era of my life—the dorm, the shows, the noise, the secrets—
ad ended.

It was time to begin again.

A few days later, I packed a small bag of clothes and some
personal belongings and quietly boarded a long-distance bus to
Konya.

I didn't know what life waited for me there. I had no friends
there—no familiar faces. No one was waiting at the station.

All I had was a name on a paper — Selçuk University, Faculty of
Engineering — and a fire inside me that refused to go out.

The bus pulled away from the terminal.

And just like that, I was starting over. Again.

The City of Konya

I arrived in Konya with nothing but a small travel bag, some saved
money, and a quiet determination to find my place once again.

The bus ride was long, quiet, and thoughtful. As the city came into
view, I pressed my forehead to the window. Konya looked old—
not in the dusty, forgotten way of villages, but in a way that carried
dignity—a city shaped by centuries.

This was the ancient heartland of Anatolia. The city of Rumi. The
city of whirling dervishes, poetry, and deep spiritual roots.
Minarets rose into the sky like silent prayers. History whispered
from every stone.

And somewhere inside that historic city was the next version of me
waiting to be born.

When I arrived at the campus of Selçuk University, the first thing that struck me was its sheer size. It felt like a small city of its own. A world within a world. Wide walkways lined with trees. Tall academic buildings stretching into the sky. Bikes zipping past. The smell of fresh simit and tea floating from the cafeteria.

The dormitory was simple but clean—a twin bed, a shared closet, and a desk. Nothing fancy, but it was mine. I didn't say it out loud, but deep down, I was proud. I had earned this space. I had gotten myself here.

I made my way to the registration office, filled out my paperwork, and received my schedule. I was officially enrolled in the Faculty of Engineering.

Then I wandered.

I walked the campus slowly, trying to absorb it all.

Everywhere I looked, there were students — sitting on the grass in small circles, laughing, reading, flirting, debating. Some played guitar under the trees while others sang softly along. A group of girls chattered on a bench, their laughter light and carefree. The energy in the air was electric. Youthful. Hopeful.

There was a kind of freedom here that I hadn't seen in years—maybe not since Hengelo.

My room and meals were free, thanks to my placement scores, but I had to buy my own books and supplies. Thankfully, I had saved enough from my modeling days to cover what I needed—textbooks, notebooks, pens, some emergency cash. I didn't waste a single lira. Every coin had a purpose.

As I continued exploring the campus, I stumbled upon something that stopped me in my tracks: the Student Community Center.

It didn't look like a typical student union — no, this was different. It looked like an event venue, modern and stylish, with wide glass doors, a stage, lighting rigs, and a sleek lobby.

My heart skipped.

I saw it instantly—not just the building, but the potential.

My mind flickered back to Ankara: the music, the lights, the runways, the applause.

This place… it could be perfect.

I imagined a fashion show. A welcome party. Models on stage. Clothing vendors, sunglasses brands, and shoe companies—all showcasing their products to a full audience of students. Music, lights, excitement. Something bold, something memorable.

While others saw a student center, I saw an opportunity.

I turned to myself with a smile and thought: Let's do what we always do—start small, observe, and then make it happen.

But first, I needed to settle in.

"Let's explore," I told myself. "Let's meet people. Get to know the faculty. Register for classes. Find the pulse of the place."

Then—when the time is right—we throw a welcome party.

Not just for fun.

To let them know I'm here.

The first few weeks at Selçuk University were about adjusting to the rhythm, the expectations, the scale of it all. I mapped out the buildings. I found the library. Located the quietest place to eat simit and drink çay between classes. I was learning the lay of the land — not just with my feet, but with my eyes.

But I wasn't there just to study.

Something inside me kept scanning, listening for the right moment, the right opening.

That student community center I saw on day one kept pulling at me. Every time I walked past it, I slowed down. I'd look inside, watching students rehearse music, organize meetings, or just hang out. The potential was undeniable. The space was beautiful. Wide. Open. Ready.

But no one was doing much with it.

Not yet.

One afternoon, I sat with a small group of first-year students near the music building. We were still new to each other, still guarded. But I listened closely, and I heard something I recognized: boredom.

There are no real welcome events. Nothing exciting. Just lectures and scattered campus activities. Most students were still homesick, still unsure of how to belong.

That was it—the moment.

I leaned forward and said, "What if we threw a welcome party? A real one. Music, lights, maybe even a fashion show, something to bring everyone together."

They looked at me like I was dreaming.

"A fashion show?" one laughed. "Where would we even start?"

I smiled.

"I've done this before."

That night, I went back to my dorm, opened my notebook, and sketched out a plan.

- Venue: The Student Community Center

- Theme: Welcome to Selçuk

- Event flow: DJ intro → Live music → Fashion show segment → Free time to mingle

- Revenue idea: Ask local clothing stores, shoe vendors, and sunglass brands to sponsor and showcase their items on student models

- Extras: Invitations printed cheaply, snacks through student clubs, and a student photographer to document the night

It wasn't just an event. It was a stage for connection.

A way to shake the dust off the start of the school year and say to every student:

You belong here. You matter. Let's begin together.

The next day, I started making rounds.

I introduced myself to student club leaders, asked professors who to talk to about venue access, and slowly gathered a small team of students who were just waiting for something to believe in.

I found musicians. A DJ with basic equipment. A few confident guys and girls who were happy to model. I wrote up a short proposal and presented it to the event coordinator for the campus center.

He was surprised.

"You're a freshman?" he asked.

I nodded. "But I've done this before."

He reviewed the idea and smiled.

"Let's give it a try."

And just like that, it began.

We had three weeks to pull it off.

There were hurdles, of course — logistics, permissions, skeptics, last-minute dropouts. But I didn't panic. Ankara had taught me how to manage chaos. The modeling agency had trained me for exactly this. I stayed calm and focused and kept everyone moving forward.

I wasn't just organizing an event.

I was claiming my space, not through words, but action.

The night of the party, the community center glowed like a small arena—music pumped through the speakers. The crowd grew. Students filled the space, laughing, dancing, taking photos.

When the fashion segment began, the room shifted. The models walked like pros. The lights hit just right. The vendors beamed with pride as their products were shown off.

And for a moment, just a flash, I stepped onto the side of the stage and looked out at the crowd.

All of them smiling. Cheering. Alive.

I felt it again.

That Parliament commercial dream. The tuxedo. The glowing awning. The music. The feeling.

Except this time, it was mine.

And it was real.

After the last song faded and the crowd dispersed into the night, I stayed behind with a few volunteers to help clean up. Chairs were stacked, the stage was cleared, and empty tea cups and snack wrappers were swept into bags. The community center was quiet again, but the air still buzzed with the echoes of laughter, music, and applause.

I wiped the sweat from my forehead, took a deep breath, and grabbed the small envelope I had prepared earlier.

Then I walked down the hall to the faculty coordinator's office, the man who had reluctantly approved the event just weeks earlier.

He looked up as I entered, likely expecting a thank you, maybe a handshake.

Instead, I placed the envelope on his desk.

"What's this?" he asked, puzzled.

"Open it," I said, smiling.

He slid the flap open and pulled out a stack of neatly counted cash, every lira accounted for, with a simple note inside: "Breakdown of expenses and revenue - our share."

He stared at it, blinking slowly, then looked up at me, completely stunned.

"You made this… from tonight?"

"We made this," I corrected him. "You gave me the space. I just filled it."

He leaned back in his chair, speechless.

I knew what he was thinking—that I was just a freshman, a kid from out of town. But here I was, running the night like a seasoned producer and now standing in front of him not just with results but with profit.

Not flashy. Just solid. Clean. Professional.

That night changed things.

I walked back to my dorm alone.

My shoes echoed in the hallway.

My hands still carried the energy of the night — but my heart was heavy. I closed my dorm door softly behind me, slipped off my jacket, and lay down on the bed. My body was tired, but my mind was wide awake. I stared up at the ceiling, the paint slightly cracked, the fan creaking gently overhead.

And then, a tear slipped from the corner of my eye, running slowly down across my cheek.

I didn't fight it.

Because, at that moment, I missed my father more than anything.

I had done something big. I had turned a vision into reality. I had made people feel joy, brought life into a quiet city, and introduced something never seen before — a fashion show, in Konya of all places. And it worked. I had done it.

But the only person I wanted to show it to—the only one whose approval mattered most—wasn't here.

"Baba…" I whispered, barely audible.

I pictured him standing at the side of the stage. Smiling. Nodding. Arms crossed, proud, maybe with a tear in his own eye. Maybe clapping along with the crowd.

But he wasn't there.

And no applause, no bright lights, no camera flash could change that.

The pain was sharp. But it was also familiar, like an old friend I hadn't seen in a while.

It brought me closer to him. In some strange way, grief became my connection. It was the thread that tied me to his memory. And part of me feared that if the pain ever faded, I'd lose that connection too.

So, I let it stay.

I held it close.

Not to suffer, but to remember.

To keep him with me as I moved forward.

Because even though Konya had never seen a fashion show before, and even though the city now knew my name, I knew the truth:

I did it for him.

By morning, word had spread across campus.

Students talked about the party like it was a campus legend:

"The fashion show was fire."

"Did you see that guy in the blazer? Api?"

"Who pulled all this off?"

"Wait, he's a first-year?"

My name started circulating through classrooms, dorm rooms, cafeterias, and even among professors. And it wasn't just recognition. It was demand.

Students came up to me on walkways:

"Are you doing another one?"

"Can you help us organize something for our department?"

"You should run the end-of-year event."

"You should be in student council."

I hadn't planned any of it.

I just wanted to make people feel like they belonged.

But now, I was becoming a presence on campus — a connector and a creator—someone who didn't just attend university but transformed the atmosphere around him.

And in the middle of all that momentum, I paused.

Because the biggest surprise?

I had walked the runway myself that night. I had stood beneath the lights. I heard the crowd roar. I felt the same electricity I once knew in Ankara.

But this time, it wasn't a secret gig behind closed doors.

It wasn't something I had to hide from the dorm.

This time, it was mine. All of it. Out loud and in the open.

After the first show, I became instantly recognizable across campus. My name traveled faster than I could walk. Everywhere I went, students stopped me. Some to thank me. Others with one burning question on their lips:

"When's the next one?"

The demand was impossible to ignore. So I went back to the faculty. After a brief meeting, they gave me a date — one month later — and once again, the venue was mine.

But this time, I wasn't just going to repeat what I'd done before.

I was going to elevate it.

A full-scale fashion show — more entertainment, live music, and even tighter execution. Alcohol wasn't allowed, so we stuck to soft drinks and light snacks. That didn't matter. The energy would carry it all.

I needed a team: twelve models — six girls, five guys, and myself.

There were no auditions this time. I had a vision, and I trusted my instincts. So, I took the time to go to the campus and began handpicking the right people myself. I wandered between the cafeteria, the campus park, and the open-air walkways. I approached students directly and introduced myself — not that I had to.

"We know who you are."

That became the most common reply.

They smiled. Some were surprised. But all of them agreed. It wasn't difficult to find the right fit. In just a few days, the team was set.

I used every free hour after class to train the models inside the community center. Walks, timing, posture, turns. I coached them like a director preparing actors for opening night. Meanwhile, I took a bus to the city center, determined to find sponsors who could help support the event.

I didn't need to pitch much. They already knew.

Store owners, boutique managers, eyewear reps — they'd heard about the first show. They shook my hand before I even introduced myself. And most of them signed on immediately.

For the first time in a long time, I felt something I hadn't let myself feel:

I belonged.

And while organizing, coordinating, training, and building exhausted me, it also gave me something to hold on to — something stronger than grief. It gave me purpose.

With one week to go, everything was moving like a well-oiled machine.

This time, I made one strategic change: we would charge a small entry fee. It was a lesson I had learned during my Ankara days: make the first event free, then slowly build value. As the name grows, so can the price. That's how you build a brand — and a following.

The day of the show finally arrived.

What we saw next left us speechless.

The line of students stretched out across campus, forming hours before the doors opened. The venue had a max capacity of 1,000 and it was clear the demand far exceeded that. We had to place people at the entrance to control the crowd, only letting in the first 1,000.

Hundreds were turned away still smiling, still buzzing, just for being near the moment.

Inside, the energy was electric.

The music hit just right. The models walked with confidence and precision. The vendors were thrilled. And when I stepped out for the final walk — just like I had in Ankara — the applause shook the walls.

It wasn't just a show.

It was a storm.

And the storm didn't stop at applause.

The money we made was astonishing, far beyond what I imagined. But with success came new realities. Because we had charged an entry fee, the faculty claimed all the door revenue. It was disappointing, but I didn't argue. I knew how the game worked.

Thankfully, I had negotiated separate sponsorship deals with vendors. From that income, I took my cut and paid every model who helped make it happen.

Because they deserved it.

No one walked away empty-handed. Not on my watch.

The next morning, Konya woke up differently.

The entire campus buzzed. Students shared videos they took with their old camera recorders, as well as photos and told stories. Professors mentioned it in class. And then, the university began receiving calls from local media outlets.

They wanted to interview me.

They wanted to tell the story.

They wanted to know how one student had created a cultural wave on a campus that had never seen anything like it before.

And somewhere in the middle of all that noise, I stood quietly, just taking it in, not for the fame, not for the profit, but for the proof:

That I could build something from nothing. Again.

The Student Who Became a Force

After the second show, everything changed — again.

The difference this time was the scale. It wasn't just a few students or professors who knew my name—it was everyone. Entire departments were talking about it: staff, faculty, even the administrative office. The media requests started coming in, and I was invited to speak with reporters who wanted to feature the event—and me—in local news outlets.

But I wasn't chasing fame.

I was just doing what I knew how to do: see possibility where others saw routine and create energy where others saw silence.

That week, I walked through campus and could feel the eyes — not with arrogance, but with awareness. I had become a symbol. Not of fashion. Not even for entertainment.

But what could happen when someone believed they didn't have to wait for permission to do something great.

I was still that same boy from the village. Still the son who lay awake at night whispering his father's name. Still the fighter who stood in a dusty market and yelled "Cold Water!" louder than anyone else. But now, I was also something else:

A student who had become a force.

Students began approaching me with more than just congratulations.

They came with ideas.

Dreams.

Questions.

"Api, how did you pull that off?"

"Can you help us organize our department event?"

"Can we start a creative club?"

"Can you talk to our professor about letting us do a performance?"

I had unknowingly become a connector — between students and staff, between ideas and action. And as always, I welcomed the weight of it. I had carried far heavier things before.

But even as the outside world celebrated, inside… I still carried a quiet ache.

Some nights, after a long day of classes and meetings, I would walk back to my dorm and sit by the window. I'd watch the lights of Konya flicker in the distance and wonder — would my father have understood what I was doing? Would he have smiled with pride or told me to be careful with all the attention?

I never got to know the answers.

But I felt his presence in the discipline, the humility, the hustle. I remembered how he treated customers, how he honored his word, and how he carried dignity in silence.

And that kept me grounded.

The momentum didn't slow.

I was invited to help coordinate university-wide events, speak at student panels, and even participate in early-stage planning for cultural weeks on campus. One professor told me:

"You've done more for student morale in two months than we've done in two years."

But I didn't let it get to my head.

Because I knew something they didn't.

I wasn't running from nothing.

I was running with something.

A memory. A legacy. A deep, unshakable pain I turned into purpose.

The Birth of Api + MORE

After the second campus show, I knew I had reached the ceiling — at least within university walls.

The recognition was there. The student body adored the events, the professors respected the impact, and the faculty saw the cultural wave building. But I also saw something they didn't — potential. Untapped, limitless potential.

So, I made a strategic decision:

The third show would be off campus.

This time, it would be mine — fully, completely, legally, and financially.

I began planning the way I had learned in Ankara, not as a student, but as a businessman. I mapped out three major income streams: ticket sales, vendor sponsorships, and snack and drink sales. I knew how much money could be made if I did this right.

That's when I met Bülent.

A local student. Friendly. Sharp. And most notably, he owned a car. At that time, it was extremely rare to see a university student with a car. He was the son of a respected local businessman, and he would unknowingly open doors for me that would change the trajectory of my life.

We became fast friends.

And with his car, everything became easier. Driving around town to meet vendors, print flyers, distribute them, and visit event venues was no longer a slow, bus-bound process. It was efficient. Professional. Real.

We scouted for days before we found the perfect venue:

A beautiful hall with a capacity of 1,500 people.

We locked in the date, one month out.

And I made another sharp decision, one I learned back in Ankara.

Tickets would be sold in advance only.

No walk-ins. No exceptions.

I wanted to create FOMO—fear of missing out—and it worked like magic.

Within weeks, every single ticket was sold.

And here's the miracle:

The money from ticket sales alone covered all my expenses—the venue, the DJ, the models, equipment, and more. I hadn't even touched the vendor sponsorship revenue or the money from the soft drinks and snacks yet.

For the first time in my life, I was holding serious profit.

And it was all mine.

The show itself was monumental.

Well before the doors opened, the city felt it. The buzz. The build-up. This wasn't just another student event — it was the talk of Konya. People traveled in from neighboring cities just to see what the noise was about.

Inside, every detail had been choreographed:

1. The music timed to perfection

2. The lighting set to enhance every outfit

3. The vendors displayed proudly in glowing corners

4. And the models—confident, elegant, trained to own the stage

At the end of every show I organized, I had a tradition:

A comedic skit performed by the models—a lighthearted finale that made the audience laugh and fall in love with the cast all over again.

And then, when the laughter faded, I would walk out—standing shoulder to shoulder with my models. I'd salute the crowd with a confident smile as the venue erupted with screams, cheers, whistles, and applause.

That night was no different.

Except this time, it wasn't a student show.

It was a signature event, and I was the name behind it.

I didn't owe the faculty a dime.

This wasn't a school project.

This was my enterprise.

And with the money I made, I made the biggest move of my life.

I decided to rent my own place.

Not just to live—but to build.

I needed a space that could function as a home, office, and studio. I knew exactly what to look for, having helped manage an agency in Ankara. And with Bülent driving me around, the search didn't take long.

We found it:

A beautiful apartment in a nice neighborhood.

Three bedrooms. One extra-large living room, perfect for a studio.

I walked in and immediately knew — this was it.

Within days, I moved in and went to work:

1. One bedroom became my sleeping quarters — simple, private, personal.

2. Another became my office, complete with a desk, a phone line, and my first real address.

3. The third I turned into a meeting room — for vendors, sponsors, and models.

4. And the spacious living room? I transformed it into a training studio.

I installed mirrors on all four walls, brought in a stereo system, and laid out the space exactly like a professional agency would.

I had built my own headquarters.

For the first time in my life, I was living alone on my own terms. No curfews. No dorm room noise. No restrictions.

That first night in my new place, I lay in bed — overwhelmed by the silence and the magnitude of what I had done.

And I cried.

I thought of my father.

I wished he could see what his firstborn son had built.

Still just a teenager.

Still in his first year of university.

No mentors. No manual. No safety net.

Just the memory of a man selling produce at a German farmers' market. Just a boy watching his father's work ethic and absorbing lessons that couldn't be taught in books.

How could a market stand guide a life?

Because it wasn't about the vegetables.

It was about character.

And somehow, I knew deep in my soul that my father had never truly left.

That he stayed in my heart on purpose, just to make sure I'd never fall.

And maybe… just maybe…

He was the one who had sent the angel to my bedside all those years ago — whispering:

"My dear… you will be fine."

That night, in my new bed, I felt protected.

Sad.

But safe.

There was only one last piece missing.

Everything I had done—the shows, the office, the studio—was real. But it wasn't yet official. It didn't have a name. An identity. A brand.

And more importantly, it didn't have a business card.

That night, I fell asleep thinking.

And in the morning, I woke with a name:

API + MORE

At the time, I didn't speak a word of English. I had no idea what "more" meant in English. To me, MORE was an acronym:

1. Mankenlik (Modeling)

2. Organizatörlük (Event Planning)

3. Reklâm (Advertising)

4. Eğlence (Entertainment)

But life would teach me later that MORE meant exactly what it sounded like — more than anyone expected, more than I had imagined, more than the world could yet see.

The sky was calling. And the sky was the limit.

That morning, I walked into a print shop and ordered my first-ever business cards.

Clean. Bold. Mine.

They had my name. My number. My address.

And for the first time ever, I wasn't chasing dreams anymore.

I was building one.

The Fall in Konya

Now that I had my own place, my own studio, and my own name on a business card, I felt ready to push the limits. I made sure to keep up with my university classes, stayed connected with my instructors, and even made time to visit my family in Ankara.

That visit home was important.

I brought gifts—clothes for my siblings, candies, and an envelope full of money for my mother. It was time to tell them everything: no more half-truths or vague updates.

I sat with them and explained what I had built: the shows, the studio, the growing business, and how I had found a way to balance both school and enterprise.

My mother didn't react with excitement or applause. She stayed calm. Her eyes held the same look they always had—a quiet storm of love and fear.

"Just don't steal," she said.

"Don't mix with the wrong people. Be honest, like your father. Be fair. And study. Don't let go of your studies."

I promised her.

"I will, Mom. I'll honor his name. I'll work hard. I'll do both—school and business—and I'll do them right."

I told her I was always the youngest among my classmates—placed in higher grades than I should've been because of my height and the confusion during my first enrollment in Ankara. It had made the early years of school hard. But now, that difference made me stand out. I was younger—but already moving like someone years ahead.

When the weekend visit ended, I couldn't wait to get back to Konya. I was full of new ideas. Hungry again.

The next year flew by like a dream.

I trained dozens of new talents. Established multiple revenue streams. Hosted monthly entertainment events with fashion shows, comedy skits, and dance. I provided personnel for trade show booths, ran live shows in front of stores in the city center, and created custom fashion segments for grand openings.

Konya had never seen anything like it.

And I had never been busier.

Then came the biggest call yet—from a prestigious men's and women's professional clothing brand. They wanted me to organize a private fashion show with high-profile guests: media executives, business owners, and even government officials.

It was the show of a lifetime.

The event went flawlessly. Clean. Elegant. Electrifying.

To this day, I still watch the video recordings. Sometimes alone, sometimes with my wife and children — to show them who I was before the world knew my name.

This was supposed to be it—my golden ticket.

I started dreaming again. Istanbul. Bigger brands. Nationwide events. A future where Api + MORE would be known not just in Konya but across all of Turkey.

But that dream didn't last long.

The show was picked up by multiple major newspapers. Interviews. Articles. Photos. Headlines like:

"Is Konya Changing?"

"A New Wave of Youth Culture?"

"Fashion and Freedom — A New Look for the Old City."

And just like that, the whispers began.

But they weren't cheers.

They were warnings.

Konya was not Istanbul.

It was a deeply religious city known for preserving its traditions, image, and identity.

What I thought was creative… others saw as dangerous.

What I believed was beautiful… they labeled as sinful.

Religious leaders began speaking out publicly.

Student groups aligned with them.

The narrative changed almost overnight:

I wasn't a student anymore.

I wasn't a young entrepreneur.

I had become a threat to the moral image of the city.

They called me names.

They said I was corrupting the youth.

They said I was trying to Westernize a holy place.

They labeled me Public Enemy Number One.

Within days, my apartment was broken into and destroyed.

I couldn't go to school as it wasn't safe.

An angry mob had formed. People were actively looking for me. I went into hiding at my friend Bülent's house. He tried to help. His father made phone calls and tried to calm the situation. But the truth was simple:

No one was going to protect me.

Even the authorities wouldn't help.

They wouldn't lift a finger — not because they couldn't, but because they agreed.

I was summoned by religious leaders.

Through Bülent's father, a deal was offered:

I had 24 hours to leave Konya.

If I didn't… I would be hunted.

And no one could promise my safety.

When Bülent came to deliver the news, I was standing in the corner of the room.

As he spoke, my knees gave out, and I slowly sank to the floor.

I stared at the tile beneath me, unable to speak or breathe.

Just days earlier, I had stood on stage to a roaring crowd.

Now, I was hiding. Hunted. Erased.

I tried reaching out to contacts — people I had helped, collaborated with, even lifted up.

No one answered.

No one dared.

That's when I realized that no one was coming.

I had always carried myself like I didn't need saving.

Now I saw the brutal truth:

Even if I did, no one would try.

I told myself:

"Just like in the village — when I was cornered — I will find my way out again. No one else will do it. But I will."

And I did.

I couldn't return to Ankara.

I couldn't face my mother and tell her I'd lost the university.

The business, maybe — she wouldn't care. But school? That would break her heart.

It would shame the family. It would undo everything I had worked for.

I wouldn't—couldn't—go back as a failure.

So, I made a decision.

Bülent looked at me and said, "Go to Alanya. It's near Antalya — a beach town. New hotels. Tourism. Entertainment. You'll find work."

Without thinking, I said, "Okay. Alanya, it is."

He helped me pack. I bought my ticket. Drove me to the station that same night.

We said goodbye like brothers.

Then, I boarded the bus—carrying only a few belongings.

The same way I had boarded the bus from Ankara to Konya a year earlier, full of hope and ambition.

But this time…

I wasn't riding toward a dream.

I was escaping a nightmare.

The Black Handbag and the Simit by the Sea

The bus ride to Alanya wasn't just a physical journey. It was an unraveling. I left Konya at midnight with nothing but a black plastic bag in my hand and a storm inside my chest. First, the long ride to Antalya. Then, a shuttle to a different terminal. Then another bus, this time bound for the unknown. I would arrive in Alanya sometime around dawn.

But this wasn't like any other trip I'd ever taken. It felt like the first time we left Hengelo for Turkey—that same ache in my chest, that same heaviness in my limbs. I leaned my head against the bus window, the cool glass grounding me as I stared out into the dark — mountain ridges faintly traced against the night sky, scattered lights in distant villages blinking like stars that had fallen to earth.

And somewhere in the silence of that bus, I drifted — not asleep, but far away. My mind took me through the timeline of my life like a slideshow of memories I couldn't escape. I was back in Hengelo, walking to school beside my sisters. I heard the chatter of my father's voice at the farmers market. I saw the clay house, the race, Ilona's kiss. I saw the wolves, the village, the fights in Ankara, the dorm, the agency, Konya, Api+More — and now… this. A boy with no plan. A plastic bag and a mountain of broken dreams.

And yet… I wasn't alone.

In that darkness, in that blur of memory, I saw it—the orange van. Not just a memory now but a vessel within my soul. That van had carried me across childhood summers, through winding roads, from the Netherlands to Turkey. Now it carried me again — not in body, but in spirit. My father was beside me in the passenger seat, silent and steady. I was no longer just a passenger in this life. I was the master of my soul and the captain of my mind. And that van — my vessel — moved forward through time and hardship, protected by the words of an angel and fueled by memories that refused to let go.

Without realizing it, my hands had clenched so tightly that they punctured the bag. My fingers were gripping something deeply familiar — the old black leather man's handbag. My father's. It had always been with me, even now. It had traveled from Hengelo to Turkey and across every chapter of my life. Inside it, I kept my most treasured things: cassette tapes from my best shows, old business cards, fashion show flyers, and newspaper clippings. It was my treasure box. My link to him.

That handbag—once used to carry passports and earnings at the market—now carried the pieces of me.

And still today, that same black leather man handbag sits safely in my office in Chicago. I built a special drawer just for it. A private place where no one else touches it. And every now and then, when I need to feel my father's presence, I take it out. I lay it gently on my desk, open it, and sift through its contents — the same old business cards, photos, the tapes, the memories. And for a few sacred minutes, I traveled through time. Back to that boy on the bus. Back to the Orange van. Back to my father.

The sun began to rise just as we approached Alanya. And with that sunrise, a strange hope flickered in me. The sky turned a golden hue. On my right, the calm, aqua-blue Mediterranean stretched to infinity. On my left, towering forest-covered mountains touched the clouds. In the middle—nestled between sea and peaks—sat Alanya. And high on a rocky hill above the city stood the ancient castle, like a silent guardian of new beginnings.

The bus dropped us in the town center. Even in the early morning, it was hot and already bustling. Tourists strolled in shorts, sunglasses, and flip-flops. I looked completely out of place—dark dress pants, heavy boots, long-sleeved shirt soaked in sweat. But I didn't care. I had one goal: find shelter. Find work. Survive.

All day, I walked from store to store, hotel to hotel, asking the same thing: "Are you hiring? Do you provide food and boarding?" Every "no" hit harder than the last. My legs ached. I was thirsty. Tired. Still, most places offered water, and some even gave snacks. That's the magic of Turkish hospitality — you're never turned away hungry. It reminded me of my father bringing strangers home from the mosque in Hengelo. "Give to the universe," he used to say, "and it will give back tenfold."

By evening, with the sun dipping behind the hills, I had run out of options. I asked for the nearest mosque, hoping someone there could point me to shelter, just like my father once did for others. As I made my way, dragging my feet, I passed one last small hotel.

A handwritten sign hung in the window:

"Help Wanted. Apply Within."

Like a lighthouse through fog, those words lit up my spirit.

I walked in, and the moment the receptionist saw me, she already knew I was there for the job. There was no hiding who I was, but I didn't care. I didn't flinch. I simply asked, "Do you offer a room and meals?"

"Yes," she said.

The position was for a dishwasher.

I smiled. "Perfect."

That same night, they gave me a spot in a crowded basement filled with bunks, more than twenty workers crammed into one space that looked like a prison cell. But to me, it was a palace. I was safe. I had food. I had work.

For the next thirty days, I washed dishes for 14 to 16 hours a day. I didn't see the sun once. My body worked. My soul… healed.

Then, finally, my first day off.

I stepped out of the hotel early that morning. Same clothes. Same man handbag wrapped around my wrist. I started walking. The street between the beach and the hotel was waking up. Cafés setting out chairs. Vendors opening stands. The breeze was sweet with salt and pine. For the first time in a month, I could feel the sun.

I was too broke for tea at a café, so I bought a single simit from a street vendor and searched for a quiet spot. I found a wooden bench near a fancy patio café and sat there, chewing slowly, gazing at the sea and the distant hills.

My thoughts swirled again. So much had been taken from me. I had rebuilt, only to be torn down. And yet, I was still here. I was still moving.

And then… as I sat there, silent and lost in thought, a single tear escaped my eye. It rolled down my cheek. I didn't move.

That's when I felt it.

A gentle tap on my shoulder.

A soft voice behind me.

"Young man… are you okay?"

The Tear, the Breakfast, and the Card

When I turned my head, I saw a clean-cut man in his late twenties or early thirties. He looked sharp, well-dressed, and confident—like someone who had life figured out. I was still in a trance, the kind of daze that's hard to shake off after weeks of darkness and a morning of soul-searching. I didn't respond at first, just stared into his eyes. Then, gently, he asked again in a soft, calm voice, "Are you okay?"

His voice pulled me back into the world, and I blinked myself awake. "Oh yes, I'm okay," I replied, almost out of instinct.

He had just arrived in his luxury car, parking it right in front of the café to enjoy his morning coffee, the breeze, and the picture-perfect view of the sea hugging the mountains. This was part of his daily routine. But today was different. From the moment he sat at his usual spot, he noticed me—sitting on that wooden bench with a half-eaten simit in my hand, staring into the distance with a tear silently slipping down my cheek. Something about my presence touched him. He saw the loneliness in my eyes and the kind of sadness that can't be explained by hunger alone.

So, he stood up, walked over, tapped me gently, and invited me to join him for Turkish breakfast.

I've never been one to turn down food, especially not when my stomach has been surviving on exhaustion and thin hope. I accepted his offer and walked to his table.

He waved to the waiter and said, "Bring the full spread." And they did. The table was soon covered with the richness of a traditional Turkish breakfast—freshly baked bread still warm from the oven, soft white cheese, cured black and green olives, sliced tomatoes and cucumbers drizzled in olive oil, fragrant honeycomb, rich clotted cream, crispy sigara böreği, jams made from cherries and figs, spicy sucuk sausages, fried eggs, and endless refills of steaming Turkish tea in tulip-shaped glasses.

Before we touched the food, he looked at me and asked, "Why was there a tear coming down your cheek?" He said he didn't mean to intrude, but he felt an unshakable pull to check on me—that maybe fate brought us to the same spot that morning.

Normally, I keep everything to myself. My pain, my dreams, my memories, my struggles, I don't share them. I've always worn a strong face for the world, carrying my battles inside without asking for pity or help. But maybe it was the exhaustion... maybe it was the 30 days I spent buried in a basement washing dishes without a ray of sunlight... maybe it was the sunrise over the Mediterranean and the ache of memories I couldn't silence. But something inside me broke, and I began to speak.

And once I started, I didn't stop.

I told him everything—from Hengelo to the village, from my father's van to the dorms, the fights, the fashion shows, the rise and fall in Konya, and finally, to this bench in Alanya. Time slipped away as I spoke. By the time I reached the end of my story, our breakfast had turned into lunch, and now we were sipping afternoon tea, nibbling on warm baklava.

The man who had approached me because of a single tear was now wiping away his own. He had listened in silence, with the kind of attention and compassion I hadn't experienced in years.

I thanked him for the meal and for listening. I told him I needed to get back to the hotel and rest before my next shift began. But he stopped me and asked me to sit a little longer. Then he reached into his pocket.

Reflexively, I raised my hand. "Please," I said, "I don't need a handout. I didn't share my story for pity. I'm not asking for money."

He smiled gently and said, "You misunderstand me."

From his pocket, he pulled out a business card—not cash—and placed it on the table.

"Jasmine Leather"

The word leather immediately triggered a memory—the factory my father worked at, the black leather man handbag he earned through years of hard labor—the handbag I still carried with me.

I stared at the card. I didn't know what it meant—maybe he wanted me to work in a factory or at a store. I would have accepted anything. Then he spoke.

"Api," he said, "the universe is paying you back tenfold—just like your father said."

He explained that he and his uncle owned Jasmine Leather, the largest leather jacket manufacturer and retailer in the region. Their flagship store was just a short walk from where we sat, but they had bigger dreams—to expand beyond the store to reach every tourist-filled resort in Alanya. Their idea was simple: send mobile teams in vans filled with leather jackets to hotels during meal hours to showcase and sell.

But his uncle had recently returned from Istanbul and shared a spark of inspiration—he had witnessed a live fashion show held in a luxury hotel's dining hall. That idea changed everything.

They didn't just want salesmen now. They wanted shows. But they didn't know where to start—no agencies nearby, no one with experience. Then he met me.

After hearing my story and everything I'd done—planning, training, performing, managing—he believed without a doubt that I was the missing piece.

He leaned forward and said, "This is why I think our paths crossed. You're exactly the person we need."

I froze. My ears rang. My heart raced. I thought of the old man at my bedside—the angel with the white beard—saying, "My dear… you will be fine."

Was this real?

Then he smiled again and asked, "So, Mr. Api… what do you say?"

And at that moment, I knew—this was the orange van again, returning to pick me up when I had no ride. It wasn't just a van from my childhood. It was a vessel in my soul, carrying my father in the co-pilot seat, guiding me through the shadows. I was the master of my soul and the captain of my mind. I was never alone.

That morning, on a bench in Alanya, one tear changed everything.

Starting Again

And I roared—just like I did when I won the audition in Ankara — and shouted, "Yes! Let's do it!"

We both stood up, hugged, and he immediately said, "Let's go meet my uncle." But there was a problem. I couldn't just walk away from my commitment to the hotel that gave me a chance and a place to stay. He smiled and said, "Don't worry. Just follow me."

We got into his car, and I had told him earlier which hotel I worked at. He drove straight there and parked right in front. As we walked inside, the front desk manager recognized him instantly and greeted him with great respect. The rest of the staff stared at me, puzzled, unsure why I was walking beside someone clearly important.

He asked the front desk to call the General Manager, and they did without hesitation. Within minutes, I saw our GM walking down the stairs in a hurry, buttoning his suit jacket—a gesture of formality and respect for someone of status. That's when I realized how well-known and respected this man truly was.

They shook hands, and he turned to the GM and said, "Api will no longer be working or staying at your hotel. From now on, he's working with us, handling our sales and marketing events at resorts and hotels."

At that moment, I felt powerful again. Another door had opened and this time, I was ready to grab the opportunity with both hands.

I asked him, "Since I'll no longer be staying here… where will I live?"

He replied, "We've been trying to build this project for a while, and now that we have you, we'll set you up in one of our fully furnished apartments. But first, let's go meet my uncle at Jasmin Leather."

Fifteen minutes later, we pulled up in front of an incredible glass-fronted, three-story building. The entrance made a statement—mannequins in leather jackets, greeters at the door. Walking inside felt like stepping into another world. The décor was upscale, almost theatrical. Staff and customers filled each floor, and every employee greeted him as we passed.

On the third floor, we approached a sleek office with floor-to-ceiling windows overlooking the town square, the beach, and the mountains in the distance. There was only a large desk and a man seated with his back turned to us, staring out at the view.

"Uncle," he said softly, "I want you to meet someone. Someone we've been looking for."

The man turned around—his face a slightly older mirror of my new friend. We all sat down. For the next hour, he told him my story, focusing on my modeling background. I pulled out my father's black leather handbag and showed them photos, newspaper clippings, and even video footage of my past shows. They were mesmerized.

Afterward, we went to a beautiful restaurant where I had the best kebabs I'd eaten in months. The hotel had fed me, but barely—meat was rare, and meals were basic. This was different. We shared laughter, great food, and even better conversation.

They dropped me off at a fully furnished apartment within walking distance of the leather store and handed me the keys. "Get some rest," they said. "Tomorrow morning, we want to hear your plan to bring this vision to life."

That night, I couldn't sleep.

I started drafting the blueprint in my mind. They already had contracts with ten hotels but no shows — just merchandise deliveries and salespeople. My plan was to build short, dynamic fashion shows: six models per hotel, quick 15- to 20-minute presentations with a touch of comedy at the end. But I needed space between tables, lighting control, and music — no stage necessary, just room to create magic. I also needed models.

The next morning, I presented everything. They loved it. They didn't hesitate to offer support. They had empty apartments, vans, and resources. Within two days, they helped launch auditions through the local community.

I pulled in 15 models from my Konya network, students out of school and ready to travel. The auditions brought in 20 more. Within a week, we had housing, a team, and a plan.

The shows launched, and instantly, hotel sales tripled. Our presence turned passive diners into engaged shoppers. It was electric.

Our events ran from 7 to 9 PM, leaving the rest of the day free. We spent mornings at the beach and evenings strolling with tourists, laughing, and learning bits of English. Life was fun again — work, money, and friendship all wrapped into one.

Soon, I appointed one of my best guys to manage things while I visited my family in Ankara. I didn't tell my mother I was no longer in college. It was the perfect cover — school was out for summer, and I told them I'd found a summer job in Alanya. My younger brothers came to visit and made unforgettable memories; it was their first real vacation. Seeing them smile, swim, and laugh-filled me with pride.

But free time can become dull. The beach every day, the nightlife every night got repetitive. So, we started a new hustle: a fake tattoo stand. Two of the models stood outside shouting, "Fake tattoos!" We laughed, calling it part of their "training."

We also handed out safari flyers. On tour days, we rented 10 to 15 Jeeps depending on bookings, and I'd lead mountain adventures — waterfalls, scenic stops, lunch in the hills. Extra income, more fun.

Jasmin Leather loved our work. Talks began about expanding to more hotels and sharing commissions. The tattoo stands, safari tours, modeling shows — all running like a machine. I felt unstoppable.

But life has a way of humbling you.

One day, I got a call from my mother. My youngest brother was in trouble at school. He had gotten into a fight, and now a group of older boys was threatening to break his arms and legs. They were hunting him.

The rage I had been suppressing for over a year erupted.

I grabbed a few friends, jumped in a rental car, and drove overnight to Ankara. We arrived at dawn. I didn't tell my mom or my brother I was coming.

We waited outside his school. When he saw me, he ran into my arms. I held his face, looked him in the eyes, and said, "No one will ever touch you. If anyone dares to hurt you, I will make this world a hell for them."

I turned to the crowd outside the school and yelled, "Listen to me! This boy is not alone. I once ruled this neighborhood, and just because I left doesn't mean I won't come back. Tell whoever is looking for him—this is their last chance."

We picked up my brother and drove him home. I saw something in his eyes I had never seen before—the feeling of being protected. The peace that comes from knowing someone will fight for you.

It struck me like a blade to the chest.

I never had that.

But I would make sure they always did.

We went home to my mother, who was surprised and emotional. We sat, we laughed, we ate. I left an envelope of money for her and kissed her goodbye.

Back in Alanya, life went on. Friends came to visit. My brothers returned for another vacation. Even Bulent, the man who helped me escape Konya, came to see me.

By late summer 1996, I had been in Alanya for over a year and a half. One night, during a fashion show, I locked eyes with a girl sitting at a front table. She was beautiful with dark hair, dark eyes, fair skin and she wouldn't stop looking at me. I couldn't stop looking back.

After the show, she approached us, praising the performance. Her gaze lingered. She was Turkish, visiting from Germany—a rare thing in those hotels. Her name was Darya.

I invited her to join us later that evening. She did. We met at the tattoo stand, laughed, and pulled in customers together. That night, I walked her to her hotel. She was kind, warm, soft-hearted. The next morning, she joined me on the safari tour, riding next to me as my co-pilot.

From that moment, we were inseparable.

She extended her trip. She moved in. She became a part of my every day.

But what she didn't know—what I still hadn't shared—was the truth beneath the surface: the orange van, the man-handbag, the weight of my past, the wounds I buried deep. I had built a fortress around those memories.

And I hadn't let her in.

One night, she wore a black dress, and I put on a suit. I wanted to recreate the Parliament commercial I had always dreamed of. I explained it to her—clumsily, romantically—and asked her to run across the street with me, hand in hand. She didn't fully understand, but she smiled and followed.

We laughed. We ran. We entered the lounge like stars in our own movie.

I felt whole. I felt like the commercial had come to life.

I didn't know it would be the last night I ever felt that way.

The Betrayal

When we entered the lounge, we saw our group of friends—girls and guys—sitting at our usual table. We joined them. Darya looked beautiful, glowing, and genuinely happy. She smiled like nothing could go wrong.

But at the table across from us sat a group of eight shady-looking men. From the moment Darya and I walked in, I noticed them watching us out of the corner of my eye. I had learned to ignore conflict—but I had also learned when to sense danger. Usually, if something didn't feel right deep in my gut, I'd move locations or just leave.

This time… I ignored my instincts.

Not even a few minutes passed before one of the men stood up and started walking toward us. At that moment, I was transported back to the market in Ankara, standing at my water stand and watching a group of older kids approach. Same feeling. Different time.

My body tensed. I didn't have time to leave—no time to act.

The man walked straight to our table, looked at Darya, and grabbed her by the arm. He said, "My boss wants you to sit with us."

In an instant, something inside me erupted. The rage that once roared through me in Konya, that had once protected my brother in Ankara… came back stronger than ever.

This time, it wasn't about defending a stand or surviving the streets.

This was about honor.

Dignity.

Love.

What followed was the biggest fight of my life—two groups clashing in a storm of fists, shouts, and chaos. I don't remember much after the first punch. All I recall is the feeling of bone against bone, blood, pain… and then darkness.

I woke up days later in a hospital bed, my body aching from head to toe. I had never been this hurt before—not in any of the hundreds of fights I had lived through, not like this.

The nurse told me I'd need a few more days to recover.

I asked her softly, "Was anyone else hurt?"

She shook her head. "No… you were the only one."

Then I asked, "Has anyone come to visit me?"

Her silence told me everything.

And then she said it, like a dagger:

"No one came."

She nodded politely and left the room.

None of my friends came—no one from Jasmin Leather. I had seen betrayal before in Konya, so this part didn't break me.

But what shattered me—what tore something in me I'd never felt before—was that Darya never came.

That evening, the nurse told me I had a visitor. My heart jumped. I thought for sure it was her. I even felt ashamed for doubting her, for thinking she could have abandoned me.

The door opened… and it wasn't her.

It was one of the salesmen from Jasmin Leather. He walked in, holding a plastic bag.

And just like that, I knew.

My life in Alanya was about to collapse.

He sat down quietly and said, "The guy you fought… he's the son of a high-level government official. Very powerful. Very connected. They've made it clear that no one in Alanya—or the surrounding areas—should give you a job. They've pressured Jasmin to let you go."

I was being discarded like a used object. No hearing. No defense. Just a plastic bag with my things.

Before he left, I reached inside the bag and felt around. I asked, "Is my father's black leather handbag in here?"

He nodded. "It's there."

Then I asked the question I feared most: "What about Darya?"

He looked down. Then looked away. And in a voice that would freeze my soul, he said:

"She's with them now. People have seen her hanging out with that guy."

And just like that, he turned and walked out.

The door clicked shut.

And something in me… died.

The next few days, I lay in that hospital bed, staring at the ceiling.

Nowhere to go.

No one to call.

No home.

No job.

No love.

No strength.

This time... it wasn't just a broken body.

It was a broken heart.

A betrayal I had never experienced before. A love that turned into a wound I would carry for years.

First Konya.

Now Alanya.

Each time I tried to build a life, the ground was ripped from beneath me.

I asked myself the question that would shape the next chapter of my life:

Where do I go from here?

The Van That Knew before I Did

Here I was, laying in a hospital bed in Alanya, recovering not just from physical wounds but emotional ones that ran even deeper.

The city of Konya had taught me not to trust people.

And now Alanya had taught me not to trust love—or at least, to close my heart.

But I didn't have much time to dwell on it. The hospital would discharge me in a few days, and I had no place to go. I couldn't stay in Alanya or anywhere near it. The betrayal was too much to carry. If Darya had simply vanished, it might have been easier... but witnessing it all unfold? It was unbearable.

Even though it seemed like I had once again lost everything, I didn't feel that way.

Because I still had my orange van.

And with it, the spirit of my father.

And the angel who never left my side.

So once again, I was going to step back into the captain's seat... and let the van take me to the next chapter of my life.

I decided to return to Ankara to regroup, recover physically, and spend quality time with my family. But I didn't want to show up like this — bruised, worn down. I needed a place to land gently before I made that journey.

So, I called the only person I still trusted from Konya: Bülent.

The hospital allowed me to use the phone. He wasn't home, so I left a message with his mother. A few hours later, he called back. We spoke for a while, and I told him everything: the hotel, the betrayal, my plans to spend time with my family. Without hesitation, he offered me a place to stay for a few days. He reassured me that Konya was no longer a threat and that people had moved on, and whatever history I had, there was now a memory fading into the past.

I accepted.

Two days later, I was discharged. I took the same route back: a bus from Alanya to Antalya and from there to Konya.

As the bus pulled out of Alanya, I didn't look back. The whole town felt like it had betrayed me. But they hadn't broken me. They had simply taught me another lesson — one that made me more resilient.

I leaned my head against the window, just like I had on my first ride out of Konya. And just like before, I began to daydream. It had become my ritual. Every time life kicked me to the ground, the orange van would return — with my father's spirit in the passenger seat — scoop me up and place me behind the wheel. No destination. Just the road. It was as if the van trusted me to figure it out on the way.

When the bus arrived in Konya, there he was—Bülent.

The same guy who dropped me off at this station a year and a half earlier was now here to pick me up. We hugged. We got into his red two-door BMW, the same car. It was a bittersweet ride.

On the way to his house, I asked how things had been. He told me the truth. After I left, nothing was the same. A few students tried to organize small campus events, but they failed. What I had started... the spirit I had brought... it never happened again.

His mother had prepared a beautiful meal. I ate quietly, still fatigued. After dinner, I went to sleep, and for some reason, that night, I slept deeply... peacefully... as if something in me had found rest again.

I didn't have a plan.

I was thinking of going to Istanbul, the biggest city in Turkey.

But first, I'd head to Ankara to be with my family.

During my couple of weeks staying with Bülent, he told me something that changed everything.

His neighbor's son, Ahmet, a childhood friend of his, had gone to study in Chicago, and Bülent was going to visit Ahmet for a month in November.

At the moment I heard "Chicago," something stirred deep in my chest.

A pull. A calling.

It felt like I was driving the orange van again… but this time, it was veering off course — tugging the wheel in a direction I hadn't expected. I resisted. I tried to steer the other way.

And then I felt it.

A soft hand on my forearm.

No words.

Just a silent, familiar warmth as if my father was right there beside me.

And he was telling me:

Let the van lead. Don't fight it.

I had been planning for Istanbul.

But now… I knew.

Chicago was my next destination.

That city, that name—it wasn't just geography. It was my father's voice disguised as fate.

And that is how my journey to America began.

CHAPTER THREE

Flying to America

We said our goodbyes with Bülent, and I took the bus to Ankara in early September. It felt strange being back home. The last time I had truly stayed there was just after middle school — right before I refused to go to the village and got sent to that strict dorm in Ankara. Over five years had passed, and now here I was again. It felt comforting to be near my brothers and my mother. Both of my sisters were married and had families of their own now, so I visited them too — though I had never stopped visiting in all these years, this time felt different.

I was going to stay in Ankara until my flight to America.

I spent those days soaking up time with my brothers. Then, I sat down with my mother to tell her the real reason I came back. I was going to America.

Just like when I told her I was going to Konya... then to Alanya... she said very little. That was my mother. She held her feelings deep, always afraid I would get hurt. But I knew her silence wasn't disapproval. She understood me. She knew that once I had something in my heart, I would chase it no matter what. Still, I needed her blessing. I looked her in the eyes and promised:

"I don't know what would happen when I get there, but I survived worse. I have my father's blood in me. I have already learned how to fight for what I want, and I believe that was enough, and I'll become rich and powerful. I'll work hard. I'll stay out of trouble. One day, I'll build you a mansion, and for the rest of your life, you'll be taken care of — right by my side."

And then, for the first time in a long time, she hugged me. Really hugged me. Since my father's passing, she had buried her emotions so deeply that it felt like she had forgotten how to feel them. That embrace meant everything to me.

Now, it was time to hatch my plan. I still had my passport from my Netherlands days, so first, I had to renew it. Then, I applied for my U.S. visa—a process that would take about a month. While waiting, I threw myself into studying English. Every single day, for hours, I translated songs, repeated phrases, and memorized words.

The final step was calling Bülent. I told him I was coming to Chicago too and that I had a relative I'd be staying with. It was a white lie. I didn't know anyone. I just needed to land. I'd figure out the rest later.

The plan worked perfectly. My passport and visa were ready. I found out Bülent's flight date and booked the same one. It was set.

November 21, 1996, we'd fly together from Istanbul to Chicago. He'd come in from Konya, I'd come from Ankara, and we'd meet at the airport. I had saved just enough from Alanya to buy my ticket and had a little over $1,000 in my pocket. That was all I needed.

As the day approached, I studied English even harder. I wanted to be ready. I had no idea what awaited me, but I felt a fire inside me that couldn't be ignored.

Then the day came.

Everyone came to the airport to say goodbye. It was only the second time I'd ever flown in a plane. We hugged. We cried. And then I turned my back and walked through the gate toward my flight to Istanbul—determined that this time, I wasn't just traveling. This time, I was chasing my future.

I met Bülent at Istanbul Airport. I hadn't yet told him the truth—that there was no relative in Chicago. I waited until we were in the air, flying high above the clouds before I confessed. He was clearly surprised and concerned.

"My friend Ahmet is only expecting me," he said. "He doesn't have space for anyone else."

I smiled and told him not to worry. I wasn't expecting anything from him or Ahmet. "I would find the nearest mosque or church," I said. "I'll take it from there."

The rest of the 12-hour flight was… awkward. I knew he was uncomfortable. Maybe even disappointed. But I didn't feel bad. I just asked him for a ride on the same plane. I was just trying to land on the right continent.

When we finally arrived in Chicago and walked out of the airport, there he was — Ahmet. Waiting with a friendly face and no idea there was a third guest in tow. Bülent introduced us, and I politely asked Ahmet if he could show me the way to a mosque or church. I also asked for his phone number, hoping to see Bülent again before he returned to Turkey after his 30-day stay.

Ahmet looked at me, stunned. "No way I'm letting you wander off in a foreign city where you don't know anyone," he said. "Come with me. I've got a couch you can sleep on for a few days."

And just like that, he invited me along.

As we stepped into the parking lot and walked toward his car, I stopped cold.

There it was.

A bright orange van.

A 1985 Chevrolet G20, glowing under the parking lights like something out of a dream. My chest tightened. My breath caught. My legs wouldn't move.

I just stood there—frozen—staring at it.

I couldn't believe my eyes. My heart was pounding. The noise of the airport faded, and for a moment, it was just me and that van. It wasn't the same one, of course… but to me, it was.

It was my orange van—resurrected on the other side of the world.

It was my father, reaching across time and space, reminding me he was still with me.

It was the memory of our road trips, his quiet strength behind the wheel, and our laughter in the back seat.

It was the symbol of my childhood, my pain, my hope and now, my future.

I looked up at the sky for a brief second. Tears welled in my eyes, but I didn't let them fall.

That van… it was a message. A sign. A confirmation from the universe that I was on the right path.

Without saying a word, I stepped inside, still shaken but somehow… at peace.

We drove into the city.

Driving into Chicago, the skyline hit me like a punch of steel and glass.

The Sears Tower stood like a black monolith, bold and dominant, reaching into the sky like it owned it. Beside it, the John Hancock Center rose near the lake—sharp, sleek, and watchful.

The buildings looked like ambition frozen in concrete. Some were old, some were new — all glowing in the late afternoon haze. I caught a glimpse of Navy Pier's Ferris wheel, turning slowly, like the city was giving me a playful wink.

It wasn't just a skyline. It was a message.

A promise.

A warning.

A challenge.

And deep inside, I knew that my life was about to change forever.

The excitement was unbearable. I couldn't wait to jump out and explore every street, every corner. I wanted to conquer this city.

We arrived at Ahmet's apartment on the west side of Chicago, just on the edge of Oak Park. It was a two-bedroom unit he shared with two roommates. Now, with Bülent and me, there were five of us. There were two couches — I took one, and Bülent took the other. We said a brief hello to the roommates, but they didn't seem too thrilled about two more guests.

We were too tired to care. It was late, and I didn't even unpack. All I had was a small piece of luggage — no more dragging bags around like in my past.

That night, I lay on that couch, eyes wide open, thinking about what had just happened.

That orange van. That moment. That feeling in my chest.

It was my father.

He was there, guiding me again. Telling me, I was on the right path.

And with that warm, powerful feeling — as if I could hear his laugh one more time — I fell into the deepest sleep on the couch. That couch wasn't much, but to me, it was a launchpad. I didn't come this far to stop here.

My First Car, My First Job

The next morning, I woke up on the couch in Ahmet's living room, sunlight pushing its way through the blinds. For a moment, I didn't know where I was. The flight, the van, the skyline—it all felt like a dream. But when I sat up and saw Bülent still asleep on the other couch, it hit me:

I was in Chicago.

Ahmet didn't waste any time. He handed us both instant coffee in little glass cups and said, "We've got a lot to do."

That day and the ones that followed were a blur of movement.

Ahmet took us from one government building to another, helping us apply for Social Security numbers, get a driver's license, and figure out how things worked in this strange new land. I didn't understand much English yet, so I followed in silence, eyes sharp, ears open. Every small task felt like progress. I wasn't just passing time; I was planting roots.

He didn't owe us anything. But he gave his time, his car, his patience. And I never forgot it.

In fact, many years later, Ahmet returned to Turkey to be with his family. But in 2025, his 23-year-old son flew to Chicago to begin a new life — and in the same way Ahmet helped me, I helped his son. Except this time, I was in a position to give him a head start 100 times greater. I got him set up with a car, a job, a furnished apartment, and the guidance I once needed. I did it not out of obligation but out of love. Out of gratitude. Out of respect for the man who helped me when I had nothing.

That's how life should work—full circle like a blessing passed forward.

A few days after getting my paperwork started, Ahmet came home with news.

"I found you a car," he said with a grin.

We walked to a small used car lot near the edge of town, and there it was: a metallic blue Chrysler LeBaron, a bit scratched, the paint slightly dulled, but the lines still smooth. It looked like it had stories to tell — and I was ready to give it more.

It cost $800. I gave him everything I had left except a few bills for gas and food. That car wasn't just transportation; it was freedom. It was the first thing I truly owned in America. And I loved it.

That same night, I got behind the wheel and drove around the city just to feel the streets. I didn't know where I was going — I just followed the lights. But I noticed something: the roads weren't random. Everything seemed… organized. That's when I discovered Chicago's grid system.

Every street was a number. Every block had a logic. Madison Street was the dividing line between north and south. State Street split east and west. From there, addresses increased by 800 for every mile. That meant every 8 blocks = 1 mile. If something was at 3200 North, I knew it was 4 miles north of Madison. This city wasn't chaos—it was math. And I could work with math.

The next morning, I sat down with a phone book and a paper map. I circled the nicest neighborhoods I could find within a 30 to 45-minute radius of Ahmet's apartment. I didn't want to work just anywhere — I wanted to work in a place where tips were better, where customers were kinder, and where I could see what success looked like.

And that's how I ended up at a small pizza restaurant tucked into a quiet, upscale neighborhood.

The sign on the door buzzed gently, and the smell of garlic and melted cheese poured onto the sidewalk. I walked in, asked to speak to the manager, and was introduced to Moe — a guy about my age, with friendly eyes and a fast way of talking. He was the owner's younger brother and was helping run the place.

I told him I could drive, I worked hard, and I just needed a shot.

He smiled, shrugged, and said, "Alright. You'll ride with Tony today—one of our drivers. If he says you're good, you're hired."

Tony showed up a few minutes later—lean, loud, Italian-American, and always cracking jokes. He had a quick laugh and knew every street like the back of his hand. We rode together for a few hours. He taught me how to handle the register, how to time deliveries, and how to talk to customers. I didn't understand everything he said, but I understood his heart. He was kind to me.

By the end of the night, Moe walked over, handed me a red delivery bag and a stack of menus, and said, "Welcome to the team."

Just like that, I had my first real job in America.

That night, I showed up in my blue LeBaron, heart pounding. I was nervous. The grid system helped, but I still got lost a few times. My English was broken. The roads were long. But I kept going.

Each house I delivered felt like a step forward. I bowed my head, smiled, and thanked people over and over. Some gave tips. Some didn't. I didn't care.

I came home exhausted but proud. I didn't just deliver pizza.

I delivered hope.

I delivered me—to the place I had dreamed of reaching since I was a child in the back of an orange van.

And sometimes… the deliveries delivered something back to me.

There was the night I delivered to an address on a quiet suburban street, with houses glowing with Christmas lights. I rang the bell, and the door opened slowly. An old man stood there — well-dressed but fragile, with eyes that looked like they hadn't been smiled at in years. Behind him, I saw a dinner table. One plate. One candle. A single chair pulled out.

He took the pizza with a soft "thank you," and I heard the music playing from inside — a slow, aching melody that sounded like it had been crying for him.

I don't know what came over me. But just as he was about to close the door, I asked,

"Sir… are you okay?"

His eyes welled. He shook his head.

"No, I'm not," he whispered. "None of my four kids came to see me this year."

It hit me like a punch in the chest. I didn't have the words in English—not really. But I told him, "If you like... I can stay for a little."

He looked stunned. Then smiled. A deep, warm smile that seemed to light up his whole body.

That night, I sat with him. I don't remember everything we talked about. But I remember how it felt.

I left that house lighter. Happier.

And on the way back, I felt my father near me.

As if he were walking beside the LeBaron, whispering, "That's my boy."

Then, there was the woman with the three kids. I rang the doorbell and waited. She came out in a worn sweater, hair pulled back in a rush, her face tired and panicked. She kept reaching into her coat, her jeans, her handbag—trying to pull together enough change.

"I thought I had it," she said, breathless. "But my husband... he took everything before he left tonight. I'm so sorry. Please... just take the pizza back."

I could hear the children inside. One of them was crying. My heart sank.

I looked at her and said, "No. You keep it. I will pay."

She stared at me, eyes wide. Then she broke down crying, right there on the doorstep. She tried to give me what money she had left, but I gently pushed her hand back.

"Please," I said. "It will make me so happy if you just take the pizza."

I turned, walked back to my car, and before I got in, I stopped. I looked up at the night sky.

I put my right hand to my chest… and nodded.

That was for you, Baba.

Maybe she hustled me. Maybe not. I didn't care.

That moment—that feeling—was worth every dollar.

I showed up to work the next day and saw that half of my earnings had been deducted. I didn't say a word. That was the cost of choosing kindness. And I would do it again.

Moe and Tony?

They became two of my closest friends.

Even now, all these years later, we still get together. We laugh about the bad roads, the late-night deliveries, the time I accidentally gave someone the wrong order, and they tried to tip me with a slice of cold pizza, the Christmas Man and the Broke Pizza Lady, and many more stories. Those were the days that shaped us.

And every time we sit together, someone always says the same thing:

"Can you believe we started all this with pizza?"

The Night That Broke Me

By now, I was settling into a rhythm, working my first job, delivering pizzas in the evening, making $30 to $40 a day, and slowly learning my way around the city. Two weeks had passed since I arrived in Chicago and began staying with Ahmet. Bülent had started school, but tension in the apartment was rising quickly.

Ahmet's other roommates made it clear we weren't welcome. One day, I came home and found they had padlocked the refrigerator and started locking the bathroom doors. That was the breaking point.

I opened the newspaper and started looking for a way out. I couldn't afford a full apartment yet, but I found an ad for a furnished room in Oak Park for $300 a month, available immediately. It was meant for students only, but I was ready to take my chances. I would've slept in my car if I had to.

But as if someone had cleared the path for me, the woman who owned the home agreed to rent me the room.

And just like that, I had a job, a car, and a room of my own.

It was the first real step toward freedom.

But I wanted more. I wanted to work harder, learn faster, and push further. I started looking for a second job and quickly found a night shift opening at a nearby 7-Eleven. It was perfect. I delivered pizzas in the evenings, then clocked in at 7-Eleven from midnight to morning. After my shift, I had signed up for free English classes—some through colleges, others through churches.

At 7-Eleven, I cleaned everything: floors, bathrooms, refrigerators, shelves. It was demanding work with little rest. But I didn't complain. I couldn't afford to feel tired. This was the grind. This was the price. And I was willing to pay for it.

Because my father had taught me one thing that never left me:

"Whatever you do, do it with pride. Respect your work, and success will come."

Whether it was selling vegetables at a market in Germany, hawking water on the streets of Ankara, washing dishes in Alanya, or modeling in hotel lobbies—I always showed up with dignity. I knew every job was a stepping stone, and I treated each one with the same seriousness.

Weeks passed. Bülent returned to Turkey. We hugged tightly, and I promised to visit once I was on my feet. I kept in touch with my mother regularly, calling her once a week. I told her I was doing well, and the truth is, I was.

I didn't feel foreign here.

Not like I did when we moved from the Netherlands to Turkey.

America felt strangely familiar — like I belonged here.

I was learning the streets and falling in love with the city. I dreamed of traveling across the country, sending money to my family, and building a future one step at a time.

But in the middle of all this survival, there was one small dream I carried quietly.

The pizza restaurant where I worked wasn't just a delivery joint — it was a beautiful Italian restaurant. The kind of place where people go to celebrate anniversaries, birthdays, or a first date. They had a full menu: pastas, sandwiches, desserts—all made fresh. Every night, I'd deliver these incredible dishes to wealthy homes. And every night, I'd wonder what they tasted like.

There was one creamy pasta I always dreamed of trying—a barbecue chicken sandwich with gouda cheese that made my mouth water. A rice pudding I delivered so often, I knew its scent by heart. But those meals cost the equivalent of an entire day's pay—and besides, drivers weren't even allowed in the dining area.

The manager made that crystal clear. He was loud, arrogant, always barking orders. If he caught a driver near the front of the restaurant, he'd scream like we were criminals. I avoided him at all costs. Moe, the owner's brother, was different. He was kind, calm, and respectful. Sometimes, when he worked, he'd let me peek in from the side and watch the guests as they dined. I'd stand there silently, imagining what it would feel like to sit among them.

I didn't want to feel invisible anymore.

I wanted to exist in that room.

So, one day, I made a decision. I would save up, clean my suit, and take myself out to dinner — right there, at the same restaurant where I worked. I told Moe my plan. He smiled and gave me his blessing.

I could barely sleep the night before. I hung my suit in the car, polished my shoes, and even practiced how I would order.

That day, I finished my shift early, changed into my suit in the bathroom, and parked just down the street. People were arriving — couples, families, friends. Everyone looked beautiful. And for the first time, so did I.

I had made a reservation with the hostess. She greeted me kindly, led me to one of the best tables near the bar, and the staff treated me with quiet admiration. They knew how much this moment meant to me.

I ordered the sandwich. The pasta. The rice pudding. When the plates arrived, I took a deep breath. I closed my eyes and let the aroma wrap around me.

And just before I could take the first bite—it was all taken away.

Two hands reached over. One grabbed the pasta. The other grabbed the sandwich. I looked up and saw him — the manager. The one person I had tried so hard to avoid.

"Didn't I say drivers aren't allowed in the dining room?"

He didn't ask why I was there. Didn't check the reservation. Didn't speak to Moe.

He simply turned around, walked behind the bar, and dumped both of my untouched plates into the garbage.

I sat frozen. My hands were shaking.

The rage inside me built like a storm. I remembered the market in Ankara. The lounge in Alanya. The helplessness, the humiliation, the fire inside me.

Then he came back. And when he reached for my arm to pull me out…

I snapped.

I don't remember the details. All I know is that I was on top of him in the kitchen, and he was begging me to stop. Tears ran down my face. I wasn't just angry. I was broken.

The kitchen staff and waitresses pulled me off. They locked him in the office. I didn't chase him.

I walked into the corner of the kitchen, sat down, put my head between my knees, and covered my face with my hands. I stayed there for a long time, just sobbing. Not because I had lost control but because the one thing I had waited for, worked for, and believed I had earned was thrown away like it didn't matter.

Was this the end of my dream?

I don't know how long I sat like that. But eventually, Moe arrived. The owners had been called. The entire staff had told them the truth. Every single person stood by me.

Even the manager, after hearing the full story, was ashamed. He begged not to be fired. The owners agreed, but only if he came to me and apologized.

While I was still in that kitchen corner, Moe came and sat next to me. He didn't speak at first. He just sat with me in the silence.

Then he placed his arm around my shoulder and whispered:

"Api… this happened because of me. I saw the schedule change, but I forgot to tell him. I failed you. I'm so sorry."

I didn't know what to do. No one was asking me to leave — in fact, it was the opposite.

They didn't want me to go. They were all on my side.

But inside me… my pride was wounded. I felt humiliated. My instinct told me to stand up, walk out, and disappear.

And then — I heard it.

A voice I hadn't heard in a long time but one I knew by heart.

"No, my son. Get up. Stand strong. Move forward. Be the bigger person. Accept the apology."

It was my father. I could feel him — not in anger, but in strength. In grace.

So I listened.

I took a deep breath, lifted my head, and stayed.

Not for them.

For him.

And for the man I was still becoming, I decided to bury that day in my memories and continue my daily life.

The Sign

The days had begun to blur together — pizza boxes, gas station coffee, mop buckets, and English flashcards. I had seen limousines glide through Chicago for nearly a year now, always catching my eye but never holding my feet. White ones, black ones, tinted windows, and men in stiff suits. They reminded me of something — of status, maybe, or that old Parliament Commercial with the man in the back suit lighting a cigarette like he ruled the world.

But I never once stopped to speak to a driver.

Not until that day.

Chicago was buzzing with another convention — something about candy. I didn't care much. I had deliveries to make and time to beat. But as I walked past Newberry Library, something caught the corner of my eye and stopped me cold.

A stretch limousine.

Wrapped in bright, unmistakable orange.

And the driver standing beside it wasn't in the usual black suit.

He was wearing orange too—head to toe.

It hit me like a lightning bolt.

That was my orange van.

Not the one I used to ride in, but the one that had carried my father's dreams.

And here it was—reborn, dressed in candy and steel, parked in the heart of Chicago.

I couldn't breathe for a second.

It wasn't just a car. It was a sign.

My sign.

Without even thinking, I crossed the street.

The Spark

"Excuse me, sir," I called out as I crossed the street toward the orange limo.

The driver looked up, a little surprised, then gave a polite nod. He was tall, clean-shaven, with sunglasses resting on the bridge of his nose, his orange suit brighter than the car itself. He looked like he belonged in a commercial — confident, polished, untouchable.

"Are you guys hiring?" I asked, my heart pounding a little faster than usual.

He gave a short chuckle. "No, sorry. We're fully staffed."

My heart dropped, not just from the rejection but because it sounded so familiar. It took me back to Alanya —walking from hotel to hotel in the heat, to hearing no over and over again.

But just like back then, I didn't give up.

"Is there any position open?" I pushed. "Anything — even cleaning, washing cars, whatever it is."

He paused and looked at me again. There was something in my eyes he must've recognized—maybe hunger, maybe pride, maybe both.

He shook his head. "No… I don't think so."

That one stung deeper than I expected. I almost thanked him and walked away.

But just then, as if something tugged at his memory, he added—

"Wait a second…"

He turned, opened the passenger door, rummaged through some papers, and then came back with a card in his hand.

"You know what? We have been looking for someone to clean the limos at night. It's not glamorous — just washing, vacuuming, keeping them spotless."

Before he could finish the sentence, I said, "I'll do it."

I didn't even hesitate. Not for a second. It wasn't about pride. It was about opportunity. About a door, cracked open — and me refusing to let it close.

"Call this number," he said, handing me the card. "Ask for Mr. Johnson. Tell him Robert sent you."

I took the card gently as if it were the most valuable thing in the world.

As I stood there on the sidewalk, card in hand, heart pounding, I looked one last time at that orange limo. It shimmered under the Chicago sun like it didn't belong to this world.

And in that moment, I knew this wasn't just luck. This was the orange van —his van—finding me again.

Not with dusty tomatoes or the smell of diesel but with new wheels, new roads, and a new kind of mission.

My father was still driving me.

Even from the other side.

The Beehive

I didn't wait.

As soon as I turned the corner from that orange limo, I pulled out the card Robert had handed me and dialed the number. The phone rang once, maybe twice.

"Hello? This is Johnson," a man answered.

"Hi, my name is Api. I just met Robert outside the Newberry Library — he told me to contact you regarding a job for cleaning limos at night."

There was a short pause.

"Oh yes, let me know when you can come in for an interview?"

"I can be there now if that works," I said with no hesitation.

Now, he paused.

"You can come right now?" sounded like he was shocked.

With a firm and confident voice, I said, "Yes, sir. I can, and I am ready."

He gave a quick chuckle like he wasn't used to that kind of answer.

"Alright then," he said. "Come on in. Ask for me when you arrive."

I thanked him and hung up.

No overthinking. No fear. Just go.

I got in my car and drove like I was on a mission — not for a job, but for my life.

The moment I pulled into the lot, it hit me like a movie scene. Limousines were everywhere. Long, gleaming machines gliding in and out. Drivers in sharp suits moved quickly between cars and offices. Radios crackled, doors slammed, engines roared — the place was alive—controlled chaos.

And it felt familiar.

It felt like backstage before a fashion show.

Years earlier, in another lifetime, I had stood in dressing rooms filled with mirrors and steam and nerves — models rushing from makeup chairs to outfit racks, coordinators shouting instructions, photographers adjusting their flashes.

Back then, we were preparing people to walk onto a stage.

Here, they were preparing machines to roll into the night.

Same rush.

Same intensity.

Same elegance beneath the madness.

Only this time, the "models" were limousines. And I wasn't getting dressed—I was getting ready to serve.

But deep down, I knew this was still me.

Not on the runway… but still walking toward something bigger.

Inside, the interview was short and direct.

"It's overnight work," the man said. "You'll clean limos. Vacuuming, wiping, restocking. It's not glamorous."

"I understand," I said. "That's not a problem."

"When can you start?"

"I'd like to start Monday if that's okay. I just want to give notice at my other two jobs. I don't want to leave them the wrong way."

He looked at me and nodded slowly.

"That's the kind of respect I like to see. You'll do well here."

We shook hands. I thanked him and stepped back out into the crisp Chicago air.

That night, back in my tiny room, I didn't even turn on the lights.

I lay down on my bed, eyes wide open, staring at the ceiling like it held all the answers.

And something inside me cracked open.

Not from sadness but from the quiet weight of what was changing.

This wasn't just a cleaning job.

It was a doorway.

A first step.

Toward something I couldn't yet see — but could finally feel.

I closed my eyes and whispered to myself in the dark:

"This time... don't let go."

And just as I started to drift into sleep, I felt a warmth around me—not from the room, but from within—a memory, or maybe something more.

I saw him.

The white-bearded man.

The one who had visited me back in Turkey at that moment when I had felt completely alone.

I could still hear his voice, soft but certain like it was meant for nights like this:

"You will be fine."

And now, I believe it.

Because I wasn't just chasing a dream.

I was walking the path my father once cleared — and the road was finally starting to rise beneath my feet.

The Grind Behind the Wheel

The first few nights at the limo company were humbling. I arrived just before sunset and stayed long after the moon had crossed the sky. The job was simple: clean. Wipe the doors, vacuum every inch, restock the bar with fresh water and mints, shine the rims, and scrub the carpets. But it wasn't just about soap and rags; this was ritual. These cars weren't just vehicles. They were stages. Altars. Private worlds. And I treated every one of them like they were about to host royalty.

I worked alone most nights. The city would slow down after midnight, but our lot would come alive. Drivers returned in waves—some tired, some laughing, some too drunk to park straight. The radios buzzed, the gravel cracked under tires, and the heavy garage doors creaked open again and again like a slow heartbeat.

I watched the drivers.

They wore tailored suits, sometimes with the tie loosened at the neck or the shirt unbuttoned just enough to tell a story. They moved with purpose. They shook hands with hotel managers, nodded at doormen, and opened doors like they were magicians revealing a trick. They weren't just drivers—they were gatekeepers to Chicago's nightlife.

And I was the guy scrubbing their back seats.

But every night, I got closer.

I memorized their schedules. I learned which cars had issues before anyone else. I made friends with the dispatcher, the old mechanic, and even with the guys who smoked out back on breaks. I never asked to drive. I just worked—and I watched.

Then, one night, everything changed.

It was just past 9 p.m. A stretch black Lincoln was sitting clean, idle, and no driver had shown up. I didn't know the details; I just knew that the car was supposed to be on Michigan Avenue fifteen minutes ago.

The dispatcher—a grumpy guy named Ron who barely spoke more than two words to me—yelled from the back of the garage.

"Where the hell is Martin?"

No one answered.

He looked at me.

"You got a license?"

"Yes," I said, too fast.

"A clean one?"

"Of course."

He stared for another second, then muttered, "Suit up. You're taking it."

I didn't move.

"I said suit up!" he barked.

I ran to the locker room. I didn't have a real uniform yet — just a white shirt and a borrowed black tie I had stashed in my backpack for months "just in case." I slicked my hair back with water from the sink, cleaned my shoes with a dry towel, and looked in the mirror.

I looked like a kid trying on someone else's life.

But I walked out like I belonged.

The ride was simple — a short transfer from a downtown hotel to a private event in River North. When I pulled up, I did everything I had watched others do. I adjusted the mirror. Turned the AC to the client's preferred temp. Got out. I walked around the car and opened the door with two hands and a slight bow. I even paused before speaking, just like the pros.

The client was a businessman in his 50s. He barely looked at me. But when I opened the door and welcomed him with a calm, confident "Good evening, sir," he paused, just for a second. Then nodded and stepped in.

I drove like I was floating. Every red light, every turn, every inch of that city felt different behind that wheel. I wasn't just moving through Chicago. I was commanding it.

When I pulled up and opened the door again, the man stepped out, looked at me, and said:

"You're new?"

"Yes, sir."

"You're good. Keep it up."

He walked away without another word, but I stood there for a moment with my hand still holding the open door, my heart racing.

That night, I didn't go home right away.

I parked the limo back at the lot, walked out behind the garage, and stood under the night sky. The wind was cold. The city lights danced in the distance. And I smiled for the first time in weeks — maybe months — not because I had made it, but because I had tasted it.

This wasn't just work anymore.

This was who I was meant to be.

The cleaner had just become a driver.

And I was never going back.

I looked up toward the sky, hands in my pockets, the cold biting at my knuckles — and whispered:

"I'm getting there, Father."

The Stories behind the Tinted Glass

I didn't become the top driver overnight.

But it didn't take long, either.

From the moment I slid behind that wheel, something clicked. I knew the city better than most of the guys who'd been driving for years — not just the roads, but the people. I watched everything. I listened. I remembered which concierge tipped well, which maîtreds expected a handshake, which clients liked silence, and which ones wanted stories.

Within a few months, dispatch started giving me the "high-risk" runs — VIPs, high-maintenance clients, and last-minute emergencies. I never said no. I was always early. Always prepared. Always dressed like my future depended on it — because it did.

And that's when the real stories began.

The Mobster's Wallet

It was a freezing January night. I had picked up a pair of older gentlemen from a steakhouse in River North. They were dressed sharp — black overcoats, expensive shoes, cigar smell baked into their skin. One of them had a face that looked like it had survived ten bar fights and still won all of them.

They didn't speak much. I dropped them off at a private club, nodded, and left.

Two hours later, I got a call: "One of them left something in your car."

I searched every inch. Nothing.

Then I lifted the backseat cushion, and there it was.

A wallet the size of a brick. Packed with cash. IDs I didn't recognize. A folded-up photo of two little boys. And a business card with nothing but a phone number and the word "Dominic."

I returned it to dispatch. Ten minutes later, the man from the back seat walked into the lot himself. No words. Just a slow, hard look. He reached into the wallet, peeled off five $100 bills, and handed them to me.

"You didn't see anything," he said.

I nodded once. He left.

Two days later, my name started floating around certain clubs — "Ask for Api."

The Celebrity Confession

There was a night I picked up a famous pop star from a downtown hotel. She had just finished a concert, and the fans were still screaming outside as we pulled away.

She sat in the back, silent for most of the ride — oversized sunglasses, hoodie up, face hidden in the shadows. Then, halfway across the bridge, she leaned forward and whispered, "Can I tell you something?"

I nodded.

"I hate all of this," she said. "The noise. The cameras. The lies. Sometimes, I wish I could go back to being nobody."

I didn't say much. Just listened.

When we got to her hotel, she looked at me for the first time and said, "You're the first person tonight who didn't treat me like a product."

She handed me a tip folded inside a note that simply read: "Thank you for being human."

The Last-Minute Rescue

One night, a driver called out at the last minute — a high-profile corporate event, 8 guests, one stretch limo, and the client was furious. No one else was available.

I was on break eating a sandwich in the back lot. Still had crumbs on my shirt when the dispatcher ran out yelling, "Api, you're up!"

I jumped in, cleaned the inside while stopped at red lights, and arrived 9 minutes late, but ready.

The client? A tech CEO from Silicon Valley. Cold at first, very direct. But by the end of the ride, we were talking about our fathers. It turns out his dad was an immigrant too. He asked for my name, and the next week, he requested me again — then again — then exclusively.

He became one of my first private corporate accounts. He even offered to help me start my own company.

That seed stayed with me.

By the end of that first year, I wasn't just driving.

I was being requested.

By name.

By some of the most powerful, difficult, and high-profile people in the city.

I was learning that in this business, being a good driver wasn't enough. You had to be a mind reader, a therapist, a ghost, a bodyguard, a host, and sometimes, a confidant to secrets that could fill a dozen books.

And I loved every second of it.

I didn't have a fleet.

I didn't have a company.

But I had something better:

A reputation.

The First Limo, the First Step

The city had finally begun to embrace me, and I could feel it. The calls kept coming in. I was no longer just another limo driver on the roster; I was becoming the guy people requested. Hotel concierges knew my name. Restaurant hosts nodded when I walked in. Club doormen gave me the kind of respect reserved for owners and VIPs. I dressed sharp, spoke with confidence, and knew every shortcut and secret entrance in the city.

But no matter how great the nights were or how many celebrities rode in my backseat, I never forgot: I was still driving someone else's car.

That bothered me.

One evening, while parked near Navy Pier waiting for a late pickup, I stared at my reflection in the glass of the limo window. The polished black Lincoln stretched beside me like a dream I hadn't yet claimed. And I decided right there: I was going to own my own limo.

It wasn't easy. I scraped together everything I had—every tip, every dollar I hadn't already sent to my family—and still had to borrow a little from a friend. But eventually, I bought my first car: a used black stretch Lincoln Town Car. She wasn't perfect, but to me, she was a queen. I polished her by hand, cleaned her after every ride, and treated her like the crown jewel of a growing empire.

And just like that, I went from driver to business owner. It was one car, but it was mine.

Now that I had my own business, everything changed. I wasn't limited by shift hours anymore. I could work as much as I wanted—and I wanted it all. For the first time in my life, I felt unstoppable. No more asking for permission. No more middlemen. It was just me, my limo, my clients, and this hungry fire inside my chest.

I had my own company, my own car, and now—my own apartment in the city. It wasn't fancy, but it was mine. The skyline outside my window reminded me daily how far I had come. I was still young and broke most days, but my mindset had shifted forever. I was no longer just surviving—I was building.

And the limo stories kept coming. Some were wild enough to carry to my grave. Others I still share as unforgettable memories. I worked nonstop. I'd often sleep in the back seat for power naps between rides, using my jacket as a pillow and setting an alarm to jolt me back to life. I carried a gym bag with me everywhere—not to work out, but to shower and clean up between jobs at 24-hour fitness centers. Going home was a luxury I often skipped just to keep the hustle alive. I always had two clean suits ready in the trunk, and there were stretches when I didn't step foot into my apartment for days.

That was the grind. Two stories from that time still stand out:

"The Customer Became the Driver"

One night, I had a wild group drop-off that ended way past midnight. My next client was an early morning airport ride from a suburban home. I was too tired to drive back to the city, so I parked quietly in front of the customer's house, crawled into the back seat, and set my alarm for an hour's nap.

I must've been knocked out cold.

The next thing I knew, airport security was banging on the window. I opened my eyes, completely confused—Why was I at O'Hare? Where was the client? Who drove here?

The guard looked at me, half-laughing, and said, "Sir, your passenger drove himself. He told us you were out cold in the back seat, so he loaded his luggage, got behind the wheel, drove here, parked, and went inside. He left a note."

I stumbled to the front seat and saw a crisp $100 bill and a handwritten receipt:

"Thanks for the ride. You earned the rest."

"The Customer Who Fell Asleep—But So Did I"

It was a brutally cold winter night. I had been up nearly 20 hours when I arrived at O'Hare for my final pickup—a businessman headed to downtown. As soon as he got in, he asked me to turn the heat up. It was already roasting in there, but I smiled and cranked it higher.

Through the rearview mirror, I saw him drift off almost instantly, sinking into the warmth in the back. Everything was still. The hum of the road, the heat, and the exhaustion hit me like a wave. Somehow, without realizing it, I began steering not toward his hotel but toward home.

My body had gone on autopilot.

I pulled up in front of my apartment, parked in my usual spot reserved for my stretch limo, turned off the engine, grabbed my things, and headed upstairs. I washed my face, brushed my teeth, changed into comfortable clothes, and collapsed into bed.

Within minutes, my phone started ringing. I answered groggily.

"Hello?"

"Where the hell am I?" the voice shouted. "Why am I in a limo parked in front of some random building?!"

It was him—still in the back seat of the limo, still asleep until just now.

I looked out my window, and there it was—my black stretch parked right where I left it… with my client still inside.

We both laughed about it later. But I never made that mistake again.

The Customer Who Fell from the Sky

One night, a wealthy businessman hired me to celebrate the biggest deal of his career. He had just closed a multimillion-dollar transaction and wanted to treat his closest friends to a night they'd never forget. He booked me to drive them all evening—from a fine dining spot to a stylish lounge and finally to the hottest club in the city with full bottle service. Everything was reserved. Everything was top-tier. He had used my services many times before, and we had developed a friendly rapport.

I picked him up first from his suburban mansion, then we headed toward the city to collect his friends. On the way in, he was glowing with pride. He kept saying how good it felt to reach this level in life and how happy he was to celebrate it with people he loved. He offered to have me join them later for drinks, but I politely declined. I was exhausted and planned to rest in the limo while they partied.

By the time I dropped them off at the club, they were already halfway drunk and having the time of their lives. The doorman gave me a nod, and they skipped the line and walked straight in like kings.

Hours passed. One by one, his friends left until he was the last man standing. When I pulled up in front of the club to pick him up, he spotted me, shouted with pure joy, ran toward me, and hugged me like I was family. He couldn't stop laughing. "Take me home, brother!" he yelled.

That drive home turned into something I will never forget.

It was around 3:00 a.m., and I was cruising on the highway at about 60 miles per hour. The stretch limousine had one of those large sunroofs in the rear cabin, and I had no idea he was planning a drunken prank.

Suddenly, as I focused on the road ahead, I saw a human head slowly creep down from the top of my windshield—mouth wide open, eyes bulging, inches from the glass. I had no idea it was my client. It looked like someone had fallen from the sky or jumped from a bridge straight onto my car.

I panicked.

My instincts took over. I slammed on the brakes.

The next thing I saw was a man flying off the front of the limo, tumbling 20 or 30 feet down the highway pavement.

Tires screeched. My heart dropped. Time froze.

I jumped out and sprinted toward the body lying in the middle of the road. No cars were behind us—thank God—but I was preparing for the worst. I knelt beside the man, trying to lift him.

That's when I heard it.

Laughter.

Loud, uncontrollable laughter.

It was him—my client—rolling on the asphalt, crying from laughter.

He kept saying, "You should've seen your face! You looked like you saw a ghost!"

I didn't even know what to say. Part of me wanted to yell. Part of me wanted to hug him just for being alive. I helped him to his feet, got him back inside the limo, and started driving again in complete silence.

He eventually passed out.

When we got to his house, he stumbled out of the car and handed me a thick bundle of cash without saying a word. When I sat back down in the front seat and counted it, it came out to $1,500.

I've had a lot of limo stories over the years—but that one?

That one flew in from the sky.

I was working like a madman. Hungry. Obsessed. Free.

The dream was alive, and I was living inside it, one wild ride at a time.

Every time I turned the ignition, I felt like the boy in the orange van again, only this time, I was behind the wheel of my own dream.

The Dream Wasn't Just Mine

People saw me on the streets of Chicago—sharply dressed, driving the latest stretch limousine, handing out business cards like candy—and they thought I was living the dream.

And I was.

But what most people didn't know was that the dream I was chasing wasn't just mine.

Before I ever bought myself anything nice, before I spent a dollar on luxury or splurged on myself, I made sure they were okay—my family. My brothers. My mother. My sisters. Because every step I took in America, I carried them on my shoulders.

My younger brothers were still finding their way back home. I paid for their schooling, their weddings, and the endless stream of quiet, unspoken expenses that come with being the one who "made it." I didn't complain. I didn't count the money. I just sent it.

There were moments when I wanted to treat myself—to buy that designer jacket, take that trip, dine in that five-star restaurant I used to deliver to—but I held back. I couldn't enjoy anything fully unless I knew they were safe, stable, and standing on their own feet.

Even after they were all settled, even after I had the means, something inside me still resisted. Maybe it was the years of going without. Or maybe it was something deeper my father planted in me without words.

Because I remembered the orange van.

I remembered how he never spent a coin on himself unless it served his family. How he patched his shoes instead of buying new ones, wore the same wool coat winter after winter, but never let us go hungry or cold. That van wasn't just a vehicle; it was a symbol of how a father moves through the world: quietly and humbly, carrying more than anyone realizes.

So that's how I lived.

Years later, I brought one of my younger brothers to America—he wanted to become a pilot. I supported him financially through a full year of schooling, watched him grind through the coursework, navigate culture shock, and keep his head down with laser focus.

Today, he flies for a major international airline. He travels the world, speaks fluent English, and lives a life he once only dreamed of. And every time I see him post a picture from the cockpit, I smile—not because I made it possible, but because he did. I just held the door open.

My other brother stayed in Turkey, and I helped him start a small business in Ankara. I invested in him not because he asked—but because I believed in him. He worked day and night, built it with integrity, and turned it into something steady and strong. Today, he's not just surviving—he's thriving. And I couldn't be prouder.

Helping them wasn't an obligation. It was my mission.

I once thought success meant having the most. But I've learned that real success means lifting others with you, especially the people who would've carried you if they had the chance.

That's the lesson my father left behind.

He never got to see us grow up, never witnessed the men we became—but he gave us everything: strength, sacrifice, service. And I see him in every act of kindness I do, every opportunity I offer someone else, especially when I hand someone the keys to their own dream.

So yes—I built a business. I bought limousines. I wore the suits. But deep down, I was always the boy in the orange van. And that van never ran on fuel alone.

It ran on love.

And if he were here now… I know he wouldn't care about the limos, the money, or the skyline view.

He'd just look at me with quiet eyes, give that slow nod of his, and say, "Well done, my son."

And that alone would've been worth everything.

The King of Chicago

The hustle had paid off. What started with one secondhand stretch limo had grown into a full-blown empire. I now owned twenty stretch limousines and ten sleek black sedans, each one spotless, polished, and operated by drivers I had handpicked and personally trained.

I had moved into a luxury high-rise in the heart of downtown Chicago, right in the middle of the action—river views, rooftop lounges, and the constant hum of energy below. From my balcony, I could see the city I once wandered through as a broke delivery driver. Now, I wasn't just part of it—I was on top of it.

The nightlife scene knew me. Restaurant GMs gave me VIP tables without asking. I had access to private events, exclusive clubs, and powerful clients. But more than anything, I had respect—because I earned it the hard way.

And then came a new opportunity.

Two of my wealthiest clients, both businessmen with powerful connections, happened to know each other. One ran a private luxury service for international travelers; the other needed high-end logistics. I saw the gap—and filled it.

I started a secondary business that was discreet and fast-moving, offering VIP concierge and transport services that went beyond just limos. It took off like wildfire. Within months, I was managing itineraries for celebrities, diplomats, and global CEOs. I wasn't just a driver anymore—I was a brand.

People started calling me The King of Chicago—half joking, half serious. And I began to feel like it. But I never forgot the path that brought me here. So, I turned around and lifted others with me.

Every driver I hired went through an Api Training Bootcamp. I didn't just teach them how to drive—I taught them how to represent. I made sure they dressed sharply, opened doors like gentlemen, smiled with confidence, and learned everything they could about the city.

Because in Chicago, you weren't just a driver. You were a guide, a storyteller, an experience.

I made it a rule: every client who visited Chicago should walk away not only impressed by the ride but educated and entertained.

And so I trained them on the key stories—the ones I used to tell myself when I was trying to learn what made this city tick.

"Do you know what 'Chicago' means?"

I'd often ask my guests that while cruising along Lakeshore Drive.

"Most people don't," I'd say, "but the word 'Chicago' comes from a Native American word—shikaakwa—meaning 'wild onion' or 'smelly garlic.' Not the most glamorous origin, but hey, it grew into one of the most powerful cities in the world. Just like I did."

They'd laugh, and that was my entry point.

"Ever heard of the Great Chicago Fire?"

I'd continue as we crossed the Chicago River.

"In 1871, the whole city burned to the ground. They said it started with a cow kicking over a lantern in a barn. Who knows the truth? What matters is what came after. This city rebuilt itself from ashes—bigger, stronger, smarter. That's when they invented the modern city grid system and the first skyscrapers. Grit is in the bones of this place."

"You can't talk about Chicago without mentioning Al Capone."

When we drove past old speakeasy buildings or the Lexington Hotel, I'd lower my voice a little for effect.

"Capone ruled this city during Prohibition. Booze, crime, bribes— he was a king in his own right. Eventually, he was taken down by the IRS, not the FBI. Do you know what that teaches you? You can get away with murder—but not taxes."

The Curse of the Billy Goat

Another story I loved telling my clients—especially when they asked about Chicago's sports culture—was about the Chicago Cubs and one of the strangest curses in baseball history.

"You ever hear about the curse of the Billy Goat?" I'd ask, glancing back through the rearview mirror. They'd usually shake their heads, curious.

"Well, let me tell you."

It all started back in 1945, during the World Series at Wrigley Field. A man named Billy Sianis, owner of the Billy Goat Tavern, brought his pet goat to the game. That's right—a real goat, on a leash, with a ticket. He and the goat were allowed in at first, but partway through the game, they were kicked out. The reason? The goat smelled.

Billy was furious. And as the story goes, he shouted:

"Them Cubs, they ain't gonna win no more!"

And just like that—boom—the Curse of the Billy Goat was born.

And it stuck.

Year after year, decade after decade, the Cubs found new and heartbreaking ways to lose. Bartman. Bad trades. Black cats on the field. It didn't matter how good their team was; they could never seal the deal.

"People used to say it wasn't a baseball team—it was a Shakespearean tragedy," I'd say, laughing with my clients.

The curse lasted 71 years.

But then came 2016. The Cubs, against all odds, made it to the World Series—and finally, finally, they won it all.

Wrigleyville exploded. Grown men cried in the streets. And just like that, the curse was broken. The city felt like it had healed from an old scar.

"Only in Chicago," I'd tell my passengers. "Do you get a baseball curse involving a goat, a bartender, and a redemption story seven decades later."

Clients loved it. They laughed, took notes, and sometimes recorded me on their phones.

And of course, the food.

"Let me be clear," I'd say with a grin.

"New York may think they have pizza—but if you can fold it like a napkin, it's a snack, not a meal. Here in Chicago, we don't fold pizza. We serve it. Thick crust, layers of cheese, chunky tomato sauce on top. It's not food; it's a commitment and it is called Chicago Deepdish Pizza. And don't even get me started on the hot dogs."

"Rule number one: No ketchup. If you ask for ketchup on a Chicago dog, you'll get banned from the city. We use mustard, relish, onions, tomatoes, sport peppers, celery salt, and a pickle. It's a masterpiece in a bun."

These weren't just jokes—they were stories. Stories that helped my drivers get better tips, make stronger connections, and become ambassadors for the city I now call home.

I had built something more than a business.

I had built a culture.

And for the first time in my life, I wasn't chasing the dream anymore.

I was living in it.

I had built something more than a business.

Until I wasn't.

It's strange how fast things can change. One day, you're at the top of the city, sipping espresso in a penthouse, taking client calls from a rooftop pool. The next, the ground beneath you starts to crack— so slowly, at first, you think it's just a little tremor. But then it opens wide enough to swallow everything.

The limo business had become crowded. Cheap competitors flooded the market. Uber and black car apps were starting to appear, and the 2008 financial crisis made it worse. My secondary business got tangled in legal headaches—partnerships that were built on handshakes started unraveling in boardrooms. And worst of all, I trusted the wrong people.

Some of my top drivers started breaking the rules behind my back. Clients complained. Cars went out with damage. One day, I opened my bank app and saw numbers that didn't make sense. I realized money had been disappearing silently and steadily. Mismanagement? Theft? A combination of both?

It didn't matter. The empire I had built, car by car, ride by ride, was beginning to fall apart.

I worked harder than ever—tried to plug every leak, cover every shift, and save every client. But I couldn't be everywhere at once. I had spent so many years taking care of everyone else that I had no energy left to take care of myself.

I barely slept. I stopped calling home. I lost weight, lost focus, and, worst of all—I started to lose belief in myself.

From the outside, people still saw me as Api, the Limo King. But behind the scenes, I was watching everything I built collapse.

And that's when fate stepped in again.

One night, after another long day of putting out fires, I walked into a small restaurant near the Gold Coast just to clear my head. I didn't want food—I just wanted quiet. A place to sit, breathe, and maybe figure out my next move.

That's when I saw her.

Karla.

She wasn't just beautiful. She radiated something I hadn't felt in a long time—calm. While everything inside me was in chaos, she looked like she belonged to another world. A world where people smiled without pretending. A world where love wasn't a transaction.

I didn't know it that night, but she would become the woman who would help me rebuild everything—not just my business, but me.

The boy in the orange van had made it to the top, only to fall again.

But this time, I wouldn't rise alone.

CHAPTER FOUR

The Spark and the Shift

I didn't expect her to change my life that night.

I just thought I was going to dinner.

The city was quiet that evening, calm in the way Chicago gets right before spring truly breaks through the last grip of winter. I remember standing near the entrance of the restaurant, hands tucked in my coat pockets, heart steady but curious. After everything I'd been through, I didn't think I could feel butterflies anymore—not like I used to back in Hengelo, not like that first kiss with Ilona behind the garden fence.

But I was wrong.

The moment Karla walked through the door, time folded. The restaurant lights flickered against the glass as the door swung open, and there she stood—a long dress with orange flowers flowing like silk around her. And behind her, as if the universe had cued it for me alone, the streetlights beamed through the windows, casting a glow around her hair and shoulders. It wasn't just a beautiful entrance; it was a divine moment. A flash of light. A vision.

And instantly, I was back in the Netherlands.

Not physically, but emotionally. I was standing beside the orange van. The door had just slid open. My mother was stepping out into the daylight, holding my baby brother in her arms. That image—her grace, her strength, the light behind her—had lived in me all my life.

And now, it stood in front of me again, only this time she had Karla's eyes.

She smiled—warm, gentle, as if she knew something I didn't. And I swear to you, in that exact second, I knew I loved her.

She didn't sit across from me at dinner—she sat next to me as if we'd already shared a hundred meals before this one. There was no small talk. No awkward pauses. We spoke like two people who had waited a lifetime to meet.

The dinner lasted three hours. The conversation lasted all night.

We left the restaurant just before midnight and kept walking. Block after block. Talking about our lives, our dreams, the weight we carried. We ended up in a quiet corner coffee shop that opened early for the morning crowd. She ordered tea. I ordered a Turkish coffee—out of habit, more than desire.

And as the sun started to rise behind the skyline, we sat at a small table by the window, hands barely touching, eyes soft with everything we hadn't said yet.

I looked at her and thought, This is it. This is my person.

After everything—the pain, the hustle, the rebuilds, the falls—this woman made me feel like I wasn't just someone trying to make it anymore. I was home.

But outside that moment of warmth, my world was crumbling.

My limo business, the empire I had poured my heart into, was unraveling faster than I could hold it together. From the outside, I still looked like the Limo King of Chicago—a fleet of twenty stretch limousines, ten black sedans, VIP clientele, and reservations across the city's finest spots.

But underneath the polish, the cracks were showing.

2008 changed everything.

The financial crisis swept across the country like a slow-moving hurricane. Corporations panicked. Executives froze budgets. Wall Street fell, and with it, the habits of the rich shifted overnight. All the CEOs and VPs I once served—the ones who booked entire fleets for outings, who demanded black cars for each manager from their suburban homes into the city—vanished.

Not the people, but their spending.

Before, one event could mean 10, 20, or even 100 limos on a single job. I had my own fleet, yes—but to fill orders that big, I relied on every owner-operator in the region. We were all making money. We were all thriving.

But now?

They wanted one vehicle. A mid-size bus. Something more "efficient." Something more "responsible."

The optics mattered now. CEOs no longer wanted to be seen wasting money. Gone were the red carpets and stretch rides. In their place came practical, budget-conscious group shuttles. It wasn't personal—it was economics.

But to me? It was war.

I hated the idea. Limos were elegance. Prestige. Legacy. I had built a brand around white gloves, bottled water, and leather seats. How could I go from stretch limousines and custom champagne flutes to diesel-powered buses?

But deep down, I knew—if I didn't adapt, I'd die.

I fought the thought for months. I tried to hold on to the old ways. I tried calling in favors, pitching luxury packages, and offering discounts. But nothing could reverse the cultural shift.

It wasn't just about the recession—it was about the mentality of corporate America. Spending had become shameful. Opulence was no longer a virtue—it was a sin.

And just like that, the foundation cracked.

Karla didn't know all of this yet—not in full detail. But as our relationship deepened in those early weeks, she could sense it. The stress behind my eyes. The weight on my shoulders. The late-night phone calls, the missed meals, the silence.

One night, I broke down. I told her everything.

How the business I built was shrinking in front of me. How I couldn't stop it. How angry I was—at the world, at myself. How lost I felt after climbing so high.

She listened without interrupting. She didn't try to fix it. She didn't offer pity.

She just held my hand and said, "Maybe this is the beginning of something else."

I wanted to believe her. But belief doesn't always come easy when you've seen empires fall.

Still, something in me softened that night.

Because even though I was facing the biggest identity shift of my life—stepping away from what I had built—there was someone next to me now—someone who saw beyond the title, beyond the business, beyond the broken pieces.

And in her presence, I started to see a new possibility. A new version of success. One that didn't come from being the loudest, or the richest, or the most recognized.

But from being whole.

The first bus I bought felt like a betrayal.

I remember signing the papers and thinking, What am I doing? It smelled like diesel. The seats weren't sleek. The steering wheel was too big. It had none of the charm of my beloved stretch limousines.

But it was practical. Efficient. In demand.

The first few jobs were painful. I watched drivers load passengers in hoodies and backpacks, not tuxedos and heels. There were no champagne flutes. No red carpets. Just hard plastic seats and group transfers.

But the phone kept ringing. The demand grew.

And slowly, I realized something: This wasn't the end of my dream; it was the evolution of it.

Because behind every bus load of managers was a new contract. A new client. A new beginning.

And somewhere in the background—Karla.

Steady. Present. Encouraging.

She never asked me to change who I was. But her presence gave me the courage to evolve.

Looking back now, I know this: The moment she walked through that restaurant door in the orange-flowered dress wasn't random. It was divine timing. The universe doesn't waste moments like that.

It was as if my father had whispered to the stars, "Send him someone. He's tired now. He's carried enough alone."

And they sent her.

An angel in orange.

Just like my mother stepping out of the orange van so many years before—light behind her, love ahead.

And just like that, the boy who once sold water on dusty Turkish streets and fought to build an empire in America… was ready to start again.

But this time—not alone.

We were Always Meant to Meet

Before I knew Karla's name, before I heard her voice or saw her smile, before I felt the warmth of her hand in mine—I somehow already knew her.

Not by sight.

But by story.

Karla was born into a life of struggle, love, and grit, just like me. Her family had emigrated from a small farming town called Linares, just a few hours outside of Monterrey, Mexico. They brought with them their faith, their culture, and something even stronger: a relentless will to survive and build a better life.

Her father, a quiet man of few words and deep character, became one of the most hardworking men I've ever known. He held a full-time job as a construction worker, pouring concrete and laying foundations with hands worn by the sun. But his day didn't end at the job site. Most evenings and every weekend, he took on landscaping jobs to make extra money. He didn't drink. He didn't waste. His mission in life was simple and noble—provide and protect.

He raised three beautiful children—Karla and her two brothers—with strength and humility. I never had the honor of meeting my own father as an adult, but I imagine if the two had sat down together at a kitchen table, they wouldn't have needed many words. They would have just nodded in understanding because both of them were cut from the same fabric—the kind that puts family before everything else.

Karla's mother was a different kind of strong. A woman with a thick Spanish accent and a gentle spirit, she balanced the home with grace. She was a housewife, yes—but also a worker. She cleaned houses in one of Chicago's wealthiest suburbs. Not the kind of wealth you see in TV commercials—real wealth. Massive homes with marble foyers, private gates, and imported chandeliers. And sometimes, when she didn't feel well or needed an extra set of hands, she brought Karla with her.

From a young age, Karla saw up close what wealth looked like—not in envy, but in dreams. She learned how to mop expensive tile floors while whispering to herself, "One day, I'll live in a place like this—not clean it." Even as a teenager, she wasn't bitter. She was focused. While other kids partied, she worked. She balanced school and jobs, never asking for a handout, never making excuses.

When her mother grew older and could no longer make it to her cleaning shifts, Karla, despite already having a corporate job of her own, would step in and clean the homes herself. Not because she had to. But because honor runs deep in her bloodline.

She put herself through college, clocking into her job in the morning and heading straight to classes at night. When we met, she was already a rising star in the banking world—managing a major national brand, earning the respect of her peers, and steadily climbing the corporate ladder. She wore power like a quiet perfume—never flashy, but always felt.

And yet, for all her strength and accomplishments, she never let go of that little girl inside—the one who looked out from behind the curtains of those mansions her mother cleaned… dreaming.

What neither of us realized at the time was that I had been in those same neighborhoods—not cleaning homes but pulling into those long, stone-paved driveways with my limousines, waiting to pick up clients for a night out in the city.

On those same evenings, as Karla cleaned windows or vacuumed rugs on the second floor, she would sometimes peek outside. From a small window overlooking a beautifully manicured garden, she'd see a stretch limo slowly pull into the circular drive. She'd catch a glimpse of the driver in the hat. Sometimes, she'd wonder what their life was like—what it felt like to drive those cars, wear those suits, and be part of that world.

What she didn't know was that it was me.

I was that driver.

I was the one adjusting my hat in the mirror, checking my watch, rehearsing the route downtown. I never saw her face. She never saw mine. But for a few seconds, our worlds overlapped. She was inside, helping clean up the remnants of someone else's life. I was outside, preparing to transport someone to the illusion of a perfect night.

Neither of us belonged to those homes. Not yet. But both of us—unknowingly—had already fallen in love with that same neighborhood.

Both of us had whispered the same dream under our breath.

And that's how I know we were always meant to meet.

Even years before that—when we compared the places we used to hang out with friends in the city—we realized we had been in the same exact places, around the same exact time. In a city filled with thousands of restaurants, lounges, and clubs, we somehow favored the same handful. We laughed when we realized it. How many times had we brushed shoulders at a bar? How many times had we passed each other on the sidewalk without a second glance?

I'm sure there was a night when I opened the club door for a group, and she walked out past me. I probably smiled and said, "Have a good night," without knowing I had just met my future wife for half a second.

We had been orbiting each other for years.

But we weren't ready yet. Our souls weren't ripe. We still had growing to do. Wounds to heal. Dreams to clarify.

And when the moment was finally right… the universe, in its divine timing, sent her to me.

We talked about our pasts more and more as our relationship deepened. She asked me about Turkey, about growing up in the Netherlands, about my father and the orange van. I asked her about Mexico, her mother's stories, her father's work ethic, and the boys she grew up protecting.

We came from different countries, spoke different languages in childhood, and prayed differently in our homes—but we spoke the same emotional language. Struggle. Sacrifice. Hope. Grit. Family. Faith.

Yes, she was a Christian Mexican-American woman, born to immigrant parents who cleaned and built homes they could never afford.

And yes, I was a Muslim Dutch-Turkish-American man, born to a market vendor who drove us across Europe in an orange van and died too young to see what his children would become.

But our hearts?

They were from the same village.

We didn't need to talk about religion, culture, or labels to know we were meant for each other. Those topics would come later—in their own time. But in the beginning, what bonded us was something much simpler:

We recognized each other.

It was as if I had spent my life building a home inside myself, and Karla was the first person who ever walked through the door without knocking.

One night, a few months after we had been dating, I took her for a drive through that same wealthy neighborhood she used to clean houses in. We didn't say much at first—just rolled the windows down and watched the lights flicker behind the tall iron gates.

She pointed to one of the homes and said, "I used to clean that one."

And I laughed and said, "I used to pick up clients from that one."

We sat in silence for a while. Not awkward silence. The kind that fills your chest with warmth.

Then I said, "I think we were meant to meet here. Just not back then. Our souls weren't ready."

She smiled and whispered, "But they are now."

When I think about Karla's father—this man who worked construction all week and mowed lawns on weekends—I feel more than admiration. I feel gratitude. Because without men like him, daughters like Karla don't exist.

He gave her quiet strength. A gentle spirit. A no-excuses mindset. The same fire that made her go to work when her mother couldn't. The same grace that made her hold my hand when my world was falling apart. The same calm that told me, "Maybe this is the beginning of something else."

And when I look at Karla now—when I see her mother in her laughter, her father in her work ethic—I realize something:

The orange van wasn't just for me.

It didn't just carry me across Europe.

It didn't just take me from pain to progress.

It didn't just drop me off in America to find my dream.

It brought me to her.

And somewhere in the unseen world, I imagine my father behind the wheel—his eyes kind, his hands steady, nodding silently as he delivered the woman who would help me rebuild not just a life but a legacy.

The Proposal and the Pivot

I knew she was the one.

Three months after our first date, I asked Karla to marry me. No hesitation. No second guessing. I had spent a decade in a city where everyone wore masks—nightlife smiles, surface conversations, glitter that always faded by morning. But with her, everything was real.

I didn't plan a dramatic proposal. I didn't want fireworks or staged surprises. I just wanted to be with her. I had been surrounded by noise for too long. What I craved now was peace.

I looked into her eyes—those calm, honest, glowing eyes—and told her what was in my heart: I wanted to build a life with her, and I wanted to grow old with her. I wanted to have babies, a home, and a future. I didn't want to live another day without her.

And when she said yes, her eyes filled with tears, and so did mine.

We hugged each other so tightly, and it was as if our souls were holding on too. The tears that fell down our cheeks weren't from sadness or even surprise—they were from relief. The kind of relief that only comes when you finally find a home after being lost in the world for too long.

At that time, I was still living in my luxury condo, high above the streets of Chicago, surrounded by the view I once dreamed of. To outsiders, I had everything—a beautiful place, a fleet of limos, access to every hot spot in the city. My place was always filled with music, laughter, and long nights with friends. But inside?

I was tired.

Tired of the scene. Tired of entertaining people who didn't really know me. Tired of chasing something that had already lost its shine. I had lived that life for over a decade, and when Karla walked in, I was finally ready to leave it behind. Not because I was running from something—but because I had finally found someone worth running to.

Karla still lived with her parents then. Both her brothers were married and out of the house, but she stayed behind—not because she had to, but because her heart wouldn't let her leave. Her mother and father were aging. She couldn't bear the thought of them being alone. She could've easily gotten her own apartment, but she chose love over independence. That's Karla. And to this day, I hold her in the deepest respect for that decision.

We agreed to a small wedding, something simple and beautiful. No glitz. No show. Just with a close family, ready to start a life. She began planning the ceremony quietly, with grace. While most people stressed about colors and centerpieces, Karla focused on what mattered—us.

At the same time, my business world was in a quiet freefall.

The limousine industry had never fully recovered from the 2008 crash. What used to be grand corporate events with fleets of limos had been stripped down to budgets and practicality. CEOs who once ordered a stretch for every manager were now asking for buses—or worse, telling their teams to drive themselves to some parking lot in the suburbs and meet a group shuttle.

I held on to hope. I told myself it was temporary. That things would bounce back, and the old days would return.

But they didn't.

Instead, something darker started spreading—quietly, aggressively, and with the kind of disruption we weren't ready for.

Uber.

At first, I didn't understand what it was. An app? A tech company? A taxi service?

I asked around. I heard stories. I joined conversations within industry circles—drivers, owners, association heads. Most were angry. Some were panicking. Others were raising money to sue Uber, lobbying against it, and stopping it from operating.

But I took a different approach.

I decided to infiltrate.

I signed up as an independent Uber Black driver, using one of my own black cars. I wanted to see, with my own eyes, what this new threat was—and how it worked.

For about a month, I drove for Uber every day.

What I discovered terrified me.

The model was simple. Easy. Accessible. No dispatchers. No reservations. No brokers taking cuts. Just a direct line between the customer and the driver. The clients didn't care about the leather seats or the bottled water anymore. They wanted convenience. They wanted control. And Uber gave them both.

I came home after those rides and stared out the window of my condo, knowing exactly what I had to do.

I had to change.

While others were still pouring money into lawsuits and clinging to the past, I made the decision that would redefine my life:

I would not fight Uber.

I would pivot.

I turned my attention to the one area of transportation that still had room to grow: buses.

At first, I hated the idea. The buses I had purchased were depressing—ugly cloth seats, rubber floors, dull metal ceilings. They smelled like high school field trips and looked nothing like the sleek limousines I was used to.

But I pushed past the pride. I began studying the industry from the inside out. Requests were coming in—church groups, corporate shuttles, airport transfers, events, sports teams. And I started noticing something deeper: there was a void.

The bus world lacked luxury. It lacked efficiency. It lacked someone with a vision, not just to drive buses but to elevate the experience.

And that's when the fire inside me reignited.

During the day, I worked with my staff, slowly restructuring the company. At night, I sat with Karla, drinking tea and talking about life. She supported me without needing to understand every detail. She never made me feel like I had to prove anything.

She just believed in me.

While others were doubting the future, I was rebuilding it. One vehicle at a time. I focused on what I could control. I learned what kind of buses were in demand, what features clients cared about, and how to stand out in a saturated market.

And I started to see something familiar…

That same spark I had felt when I bought my first limo.

That same hunger. That same vision. That same why.

But this time, I wasn't alone.

Karla was by my side. Quietly cheering me on. Reminding me who I was.

People say falling in love is like floating.

For me, it was anchoring.

Karla gave me a place to land. A reason to slow down. A deeper purpose to rise again.

And the timing couldn't have been more divine.

Because just as Uber was rewriting the playbook for car services, I was quietly building a new empire behind the scenes. Not a flash-in-the-pan business. Not a comeback for attention. But a long-term vision for what was next.

There's a kind of peace that comes from knowing you've already lived one dream—and now you get to build another with someone you love.

I still remember the nights when I'd walk into my condo after a long day, and Karla would already be there—feet tucked under her on the couch, laptop open, planning our wedding while I reviewed bus specs. We were two immigrants' children, raised on sacrifice and struggle, now planning a future built not just on survival but intention.

And in those quiet moments, I would think:

This is what my father dreamed of.

Not the buses. Not the money. Not even the success.

But this feeling.

Love. Purpose. Direction.

The Birth of Infinity

We got married about two months after I proposed. It wasn't a grand event with hundreds of guests or flashing cameras—it was simple, warm, and deeply personal. A small ceremony attended by Karla's parents, her brothers, a few cousins, and my two sisters. My mother couldn't come; her health had worsened, and my brothers stayed behind in Turkey to care for her. I missed them deeply that day. But more than anything, I missed him—my father. I looked up to the sky during our vows, the sun casting a golden hue over the ceremony, and I whispered in my heart, "I wish you were here, Baba. But I know you're watching."

The wedding was emotional and beautiful. As Karla walked toward me, her eyes glistening with joy, I felt a peace I hadn't known before. There was something divine in the way she looked at me as if she already knew the life we were going to build together. When we exchanged vows, our voices trembled with tears, and when we kissed as husband and wife, I could almost hear the gentle applause of those who couldn't be there in person but lived on in spirit.

That same year, she got pregnant. When she told me, I froze. Not because I was scared but because my heart swelled so full it felt like it would burst. I placed my ear gently against her belly and whispered, "Welcome, my little one."

When my son was born, I was the first to hold him. My hands, almost moving on their own, raised him gently toward the sky as if presenting him to my father. I looked into his tiny eyes and whispered, "To honor you, Baba, I will name him after you." And in that moment, I broke. Tears poured down uncontrollably—tears of love, of loss, of a circle being completed. It was as if my heart and soul were cheering in unison. My father wasn't gone—he had returned, in the form of my son.

I gently passed our newborn to Karla, and as she cradled him against her chest, we both cried, overwhelmed by the love that filled the room. It was the purest moment of my life.

Karla's mother came over and hugged me. Her English was limited, but her heart spoke volumes. With her warm smile, she looked into my eyes and said in Spanish,

"El bebé traerá pan."

"The baby will bring bread."

She knew. She had seen the struggle, the sleepless nights, the weight I carried behind my smile. And somehow, her words were a blessing. That baby didn't just bring love—he brought life, momentum, and something I hadn't had in years: balance.

Around the same time, my business was undergoing a transformation. We were steadily stepping away from the limousine industry and moving into mid-size buses. By the end of that year, we had sold off every last limo and black car. What remained was a fleet of about twenty buses, all different makes and models, each one a stepping stone toward a new future.

My sales team worked miracles. They shifted the identity of our company from a luxury car service to a professional transportation provider. We still offered limo services through trusted partners, but our buses—our own fleet—became the beating heart of our business.

And wouldn't you know it? Karla's mother was right. After the baby was born, something shifted as if the universe had opened a door. Our phones wouldn't stop ringing. Business took off like wildfire. But something about the buses bothered me. They were all different on the outside—different bodies, different interiors. I wanted consistency, identity, and class.

So, we invested again. We removed all the old cloth seats, the worn rubber floors, and the dull wall panels. We redesigned the interiors with elegant lighting, plush seating, sleek finishes, sound systems, and TVs. We transformed ordinary buses into luxury rides. For the first time, I looked at my fleet and smiled. They didn't just move people; they represented us.

But just as I began to feel confident in our direction, new challenges rolled in with the weight of diesel engines.

As demand increased, especially from larger groups, we were pushed to expand beyond our mid-size buses. Our 38-passenger buses couldn't accommodate certain clients, and we needed full-size motorcoaches—those giants that hold 56 passengers and carry massive luggage compartments underneath.

We took a bold step and ordered ten of them.

Around that same time, my daughter was born. My gem. My soul. Her arrival was just as divine as her brother's. Karla had always wanted to honor her mother, and so we named our daughter after her. When I held her for the first time, I felt a different kind of emotion—a gentler love, like calm waves lapping against a quiet shore. She didn't cry; she just looked at me with those dark, curious eyes. I whispered, "I will protect you for as long as I live."

And again, Karla's mother smiled and said, "The baby brought bread again."

And she was right. The new motorcoaches helped us land big contracts. Our business bloomed.

With our second child, our priorities began to shift. We moved out of our downtown place and rented a modern townhome in the suburbs, close to Karla's parents. It was quiet, safe, and filled with the kind of warmth only family neighborhoods carry. We began to look for land near our dream neighborhood—somewhere we could build a forever home for our growing family.

But growth doesn't come without pain.

The new motorcoaches were beautiful, yes—but they were a nightmare to maintain. Each one costs four to five times more than a mid-size bus. They required specialized technicians and expensive parts, and none of the major components were made in America. Parts would take weeks—sometimes months—to arrive. We had buses sitting idle, costing us thousands just in downtime. The midsize buses were built on American-made chassis and modified by local builders, which gave us options. But even those weren't standardized. From the outside, every bus looked different.

I had built a strong revenue stream, but I didn't feel settled. Something felt unfinished. I tried to ignore it, telling myself that everyone in the industry accepted this chaos. But deep down, I craved unity—something that would tie all this together. I wanted a brand, an identity, a name that meant something.

So, I began thinking about rebranding.

Weeks passed. Nothing felt right. I would jot down names at night, stare at bus photos, and brainstorm with my team—but nothing stuck.

Then, one night, after putting the kids to bed, Karla and I sat on the couch, sipping tea and catching up. We started talking about how far we'd come, from the old limo days to now running dozens of buses across the region. Karla smiled gently and said,

"Wouldn't it be amazing if your father was here in his orange van to see what you've built? Imagine him looking at all your large white vans!"

She had meant to say "buses," but in her gentle slip—vans—something stirred in me. My chest tightened, and a tear welled up in the corner of my eye.

The orange van.

The orange van.

The one that took me across countries, through childhood, through grief and laughter. The van that symbolizes movement, family, and dreams.

It hit me like lightning.

Infinity.

I stood up and said it aloud:

"Infinity."

That was it. That was the name.

Because the orange van had never stopped moving, even after all these years, even after losing my father, even after changing countries and careers—it was still carrying me forward. Spiritually, emotionally, eternally. Infinity was the only word that could hold the weight of that journey.

Within a month, we redesigned the entire brand. The white buses were wrapped with orange accents. Our logo was a sleek, modern infinity symbol—our new name: Infinity Transportation Management.

Now, I didn't just have a fleet of buses. I had an army of orange vans moving across Chicago—each one echoing the memory of my father and the promise I made as a boy.

But something still gnawed at me. A whisper inside. The buses looked beautiful, but the headaches didn't stop. I couldn't keep managing a fleet where no two vehicles were the same under the hood. My vision wasn't complete yet.

And that's when my persistence took over.

I wasn't going to be just another transportation company. I was going to build the most innovative, visionary, and unified fleet in the industry.

And I was just getting started.

The Super Coach and the Stone Mansion

In 2017, we were blessed with the birth of our third child—a boy.

But this wasn't just any birth. It was different. He came into this world with eyes wide open and a quiet strength. He didn't cry.

The room stood still. Doctors and nurses waited for the sound of his voice, but he remained silent, calm, almost as if to say, "Don't worry, I'm ready for this."

He didn't need to cry to make his presence known—he was born with a fire in his soul. And I felt it. When I held him in my arms for the first time, I didn't hear a scream—I felt a storm settling. Like the final piece of a puzzle had clicked into place.

With his birth came a surge of new energy. Something unexplainable. I had been fighting battles on every front—business, identity, ambition—but his arrival realigned everything. I looked at Karla, tired but glowing, and we both knew this was a new chapter.

A week later, as if it were written in the stars, Karla found the perfect land in the neighborhood we had dreamed about for years. It was tucked into rolling hills, surrounded by towering trees, and offered enough space for our kids to grow freely. She immediately took the reins. While caring for a newborn, she began designing our forever home. Every night, after nursing and rocking the baby to sleep, she would sit with architectural sketches, and contractor estimates spread across the dining table. Brick by brick, she was building our dream.

And I—well, I was building something too.

I found myself thinking back to that clay house I molded as a boy in Hengelo. That tiny sculpture I made for my father in our garden, shaping each wall with love and focus, only to hear him say:

"You're going to be a builder."

For years, I thought he meant buildings—homes, maybe even towers. But now, I understood. My calling wasn't stone or concrete. It was motion. It was an innovation. I wasn't meant to build places for people to stay—I was meant to build how they move.

So, I took a leap.

I had a vision for a new kind of bus. A bus that didn't look like the outdated giants we'd been forced to buy. I imagined something sleeker, more modern, more efficient. An aerodynamic design made entirely in the United States. A coach that looked luxurious but was affordable. Durable. Easy to maintain. A true alternative to the bulky, breakdown-prone monsters we had dealt with for years.

I started knocking on doors. I set up meetings with every single bus builder in the country. I pitched my idea to CEOs and plant managers—drawings, specs, and market data. But time and again, I was told the same thing:

"This won't work."

"Too risky."

"Stick to what's proven."

But I didn't give up.

Eventually, someone mentioned a name: David. A legend in the industry. He had built the world's largest limousine manufacturing company, headquartered in Springfield, Missouri, with a secondary operation in Riverside, California.

But like the limo business itself, David's empire had taken a hit. The limousine industry was crumbling. His manufacturing plants were struggling. The timing was perfect—for both of us.

I reached out. We set up a meeting.

When I met David, it was like meeting an older version of myself. He listened—really listened—as I laid out my vision. And then I saw it: that spark in his eyes. The same spark I had seen in my father's eyes when I showed him that clay house.

We were both builders at heart—dreamers who had been pushed to the edge and now meeting at the perfect time.

David said yes.

Together, we began what would become a game-changer in the U.S. transportation industry.

We named it SuperCoach—a bold, sleek, fully reimagined full-size coach that had the aerodynamic look of a European bus, the power of an American chassis, and the comfort of luxury travel. It was lighter, cheaper to maintain, and built for efficiency without sacrificing class.

I placed an order for 50 brand-new SuperCoaches.

For the first time in U.S. bus industry history, a fleet was being purpose-built—assembled from various parts and engineered as a vision. Production began in 2017, and we received the first batch in late 2018. The rest rolled in steadily through 2019.

As each SuperCoach arrived, we sold off our older, inconsistent buses. By the end of 2019, Infinity Transportation Management had a uniform fleet of 50 SuperCoaches—all identical in design, all wrapped in our signature orange and white, all carrying the spirit of that orange van from my childhood.

The marketing team worked relentlessly that year. We filmed campaigns, revamped our website, and sent press releases. The reaction was explosive. Clients loved the new look. Our operational costs dropped. Maintenance was simplified. And most importantly, our bottom line soared.

With that growth, we gave back.

Drivers' pay went up. Staff salaries increased. We hosted appreciation events. We became the dream company for which to work in Chicagoland. Drivers who once bounced between companies now stayed with us—loyal, proud, and part of something bigger.

While I reshaped the fleet, Karla continued pouring her soul into our home. It took nearly two years of her unwavering focus, grit, and talent. Every tile, every window, every doorknob had her fingerprint. She worked with architects, negotiated with contractors, and sometimes even stood in the mud, measuring foundation lines herself.

And when it was finally done… we moved in.

Our dream home. Built on 1.5 acres. Three stories, carved from stone, standing slightly taller than any other house in the neighborhood—not out of pride, but as a quiet testament to what was possible.

In the back, we built an expansive patio and a pool that shimmered under the summer sun. The kids ran barefoot through the grass. The rooms echoed with laughter. And for the first night in our new home, all five of us—me, Karla, and our three children—slept in the same bed, wrapped in blankets, tangled in joy.

We had seen other homes like this. Karla had cleaned some of them growing up. I had picked up customers from them for years. They always felt so far away—like something for other people.

But now, we were here.

We were no longer dreaming in them.

We were sleeping in one.

I couldn't explain the feeling. It wasn't just happiness. It was vindication. From Hengelo to Sarıkaya. From Alanya to Chicago. From pizza delivery to SuperCoach.

This was it. This was our new beginning.

The year 2020 was on the horizon.

We had three healthy children.

We had our own mansion.

We had a newly designed, 50-unit, uniform fleet.

We had made it.

Did we?

And just as we felt the warmth of the mountaintop…

the clouds began to gather.

The Collapse That Didn't Win

By the end of 2019, Infinity Transportation was not just a company. It was a name that echoed across the industry. We had made it.

Our SuperCoaches were a hit. Sleek, uniform, and unmistakable on the road. We had finally become what I had always dreamed of—a fleet not just running routes but redefining the standard.

We were featured in magazines. Podcasts invited me to share our story. Articles were written with headlines like "The Future of Group Travel Is Here." Our branding was everywhere. Clients were loyal. Competitors were watching.

And at home? Peace.

We were enjoying the new mansion—our dream realized. Three children growing strong. Laughter in the hallways. The fireplace glows at night. Even my mother, thousands of miles away in Ankara, was finally settled. I had bought her a beautiful home, surrounded her with comfort, and hired a full-time caretaker. She was happy. My siblings were thriving. Karla's parents were proud. Everything felt aligned.

I remember lying in bed one night, staring at the ceiling, thinking: We are unstoppable.

And then—

The world stopped.

Covid.

It came like a silent wave and drowned everything.

One week, we were scaling routes and finalizing contracts. The next, the streets were empty. Events canceled. Offices closed. Schools shut down. The world locked its doors.

Buses stopped moving.

No movement meant no revenue.

And in this business, no revenue is a death sentence.

At first, like many others, I thought—Maybe a few weeks—a brief pause. We'll be back on the road in no time.

But weeks became months—extension after extension. No clarity. No control.

Sleepless nights began.

I wasn't just a businessman—I was a husband and a father. Karla had left her corporate job after our second child to help build our dream. We had placed everything on this business—our income, future, and faith.

And now?

Now, I was watching people I loved lose everything.

Friends and fellow entrepreneurs—one by one, they closed their businesses. Restaurants, salons, event companies, competitors. One after another, the lights went out. Some of those lights would never come back on.

But I couldn't afford to panic. I had to fight.

Thankfully, I had learned from past failures. After our earlier losses, I had built a financial cushion—a survival reserve. We had enough to keep the company afloat for 18 months if we budgeted tightly and sacrificed early.

We made the hardest decision first:

Let go of all our drivers.

Not because they failed us—but because we had nothing to give them. It broke my heart.

We kept only our core leadership team—the managers and directors who had stood with me through every storm. We kept them on full salary. Not because it was easy but because I believed in loyalty, and I knew they were the soul of Infinity.

Each month, we burned through savings—hoping, praying this would end. But as the 18-month mark approached, I saw the writing on the wall.

We were running out of time.

I sat down with Karla.

My voice cracked as I told her we had two choices:

- Sell the house and try to keep the company alive a little longer.

- Accept defeat. Close the doors. Walk away.

Before I even finished, she reached for my hand.

With tears in her eyes, she said,

"We got this, Api. I'd rather live in a shed and see you happy. I trust you."

That moment—right there—is what real love looks like, not just through smiles and successes but through fear, sacrifice, and the unknown.

The next day, she started looking for modest homes. She even contacted a realtor to prepare our mansion for listing—the very house she had spent years designing, room by room.

I promised her: I will build you another. Better. One day.

I prepared to break the news to our leadership team.

When I gathered them, I tried to hold it together. I told them the truth. I told them the dream might be ending.

Some of them cried. Others just nodded. Some came up to me silently and hugged me. They knew.

But then something happened I'll never forget.

They had already talked among themselves. And they decided.

They weren't going anywhere.

They would continue showing up every day—without pay—for two more months.

Not because they had work.

Not because there was money.

But because they believed. In me. In Infinity. In us.

So that's exactly what they did.

Every morning, they arrived. They sat in the office. Checked the buses. Turned on engines. Walked the lots. Made sure the wheels didn't rust, just in case.

We weren't operating. But we were breathing.

Their loyalty gave me two more months of life.

Two more months of hope.

So, I couldn't waste it.

I pulled out the only thing I had left: my old hustle.

I signed up as a black car Uber driver.

I started working in hotels. Downtown. Lounges. Airports.

Anywhere there was movement—I chased it.

I was back on the streets, like in the early days. Sometimes I didn't come home. I would nap in the car. Eat from convenience stores. Refuel with vending machine coffee.

Not because I needed the income.

But because I needed to prove—to myself, to my team, to my family—that I wasn't done.

I wasn't going to watch the last two months of our lifeline fade without a fight.

And then, almost like a scene written by fate…

It happened.

Just days before our final deadline—restrictions were lifted.

The phones rang.

Emails poured in.

Clients were booking.

Demand surged.

Infinity had survived.

Not because we were lucky.

But because we had loyalty.

Because we had faith.

Because we had grit.

The world had stopped.

But we never let the engine die.

Back on the Road, Toward Home

When the world reopened, it didn't happen all at once. It came in whispers, then in waves. The first few clients were cautious. Events returned slowly. People hesitated to shake hands again.

But for Infinity Transportation, it was enough.

We were back.

Not just functioning—thriving.

We'd made it to the other side.

The Recovery

I didn't flip a switch and go back to "business as usual." I couldn't.

I wasn't the same man anymore.

COVID had stripped away the illusions. I had stared at the edge— prepared to lose everything. And I came out knowing what really mattered.

We restructured operations—streamlined systems, cut the waste, and doubled down on the team that stayed with me through the storm.

Our managers weren't just employees anymore—they were family.

And they knew it.

I gave them more autonomy. More ownership. More respect. Because they earned it not with spreadsheets but with loyalty.

We also reevaluated who we served. The world had changed, and so had transportation: more group travel, more corporate shuttles, more local tourism. Our SuperCoaches were suddenly in high demand—not just for style, but for practicality. Affordable. Clean. Safe. Uniform.

Infinity became a symbol of reliability in uncertain times.

Clients weren't just booking rides—they were booking trust.

And slowly, month by month, revenue returned.

Stronger. Smarter. Cleaner.

The Lessons

What COVID took from me, it also gave.

It reminded me:

- That success without a soul is empty.

- That loyalty is worth more than strategy.

- That love—true love, like Karla's—is the ultimate wealth.

- And that the spirit of my father never left me. Not in the mansion, not in the buses, not in the black car that I drove through empty streets.

It lived in every sacrifice. Every comeback. Every mile.

The Decision

By late 2021, Infinity was fully operational again.

And I needed something else—not for the business, but for my soul.

And now, with our children growing fast, I knew it was time.

Time to take them not just on a vacation—but on a journey.

A journey through the roads that shaped me.

A journey through stories I had carried alone for far too long.

So, we packed our bags.

This time, I wasn't alone.

Karla was by my side.

And our three children—wide-eyed, full of curiosity—were finally ready to see where it all began.

The Journey to Past

Before heading to Turkey, before the graveyard in Sarıkaya, before the winding roads to Alanya and the wreckage of my father's gas station… there was Hengelo, where everything began—a place my soul never truly left.

The Netherlands. Hengelo.

We landed quietly in Amsterdam, and after the usual shuffle of airport lines and baggage claims, we rented a car and drove east — past windmills, blooming fields, and tidy roads that looked like they had been trimmed by angels. It was strange how familiar it all still felt, as if time had slowed down just for me.

The moment we turned into Hengelo, something in me broke wide open.

I wasn't the father anymore. I wasn't the man running a multimillion-dollar business in Chicago. I wasn't even the immigrant who had fought tooth and nail through Turkey and America. I was just Api — the boy with wild hair and scraped knees who used to race his sisters through the gardens and ride his bike to school along the creek.

My kids sat in silence as I pulled up to the small street where our house once stood.

"There," I said, my voice barely coming out. "That's the garden we used to run through. That's the path to school. That's where your aunt first showed me how to ride a bike."

The house was still there. Smaller than I remembered. But the garden—the garden felt eternal. The hedges weren't as tall, and the flowers had changed, but I swear, I could still smell the earth from the day I dug a hole trying to plant a candy wrapper.

We walked toward the school—the same walk I used to take, holding my older sister's hand. We crossed the little bridge by the creek. I showed them the bakery, where the smell of fresh bread used to make me dizzy with joy. We ate Patat together. I told them about the playground, about the day I kissed Ilona, and about the night I learned my father was dying.

I knelt down in front of my kids and said, "This is where I first knew happiness. Before pain. Before grief. This is where your Baba was born—not in a hospital, but in the laughter of these streets."

Karla reached for my hand, and I could feel the tears pooling in her eyes too. She didn't need to speak. She felt it—the gravity of the soil beneath our feet.

That night, we stayed in a small hotel in town. I barely slept. I walked the streets alone for a while, retracing old routes, hearing echoes of my father's voice… the way he'd yell from the Orange van for us to get in or how he'd call out to customers in Dutch, Turkish, and broken German all at once.

And just before sunrise, I sat on a bench outside that same market square where he once sold vegetables. I closed my eyes and whispered, "Baba… I came back. I brought them here. They know now. They know who we were."

That moment—the first time I returned to where it all began—was the full circle I didn't know I needed.

From there, we flew to Turkey… carrying not just luggage but the ghosts of laughter, of lessons, of love that never left.

We flew from Amsterdam to Istanbul and, from there, caught a connecting flight to Fethiye—a coastal paradise on Turkey's southwest edge.

There, under a bright Mediterranean sun, we rented a van. A plain white van. Nothing fancy. But to me, it felt like a time machine.

As I took the driver's seat, a strange silence fell over me. The hum of the engine reminded me of my father's orange van. I looked back through the rearview mirror and saw my children laughing, my wife settling them in—and I felt something ancient awaken inside me.

We were going home.

The Coastline Drive–Fethiye to Alanya

The drive along the Turkish Riviera is nothing short of divine.

We hugged the coastline—blue waves dancing beside us, cliffs rising above us. The roads were narrow in places, winding like veins through lush green hills, olive groves, and sleepy fishing villages.

We passed Kaş, with its whitewashed houses and diving spots carved into history. I told my kids about the Lycian tombs carved into the rock walls. We pulled over in Demre to visit the Church of St. Nicholas—yes, Santa Claus came from this soil.

In Antalya, we stopped to explore the ancient Roman harbor, where old stone meets turquoise sea. My son stood inside the ruins of Hadrian's Gate while I explained how empires once rose and fell where he now stood.

As we neared Alanya, I grew quieter. Memories were swelling.

This was where I once washed dishes in a hotel basement, where I lived in silence, pain, and pride, where my story took its first adult turn.

We stayed a night near the harbor. I took my children up to Alanya Castle—high above the city, looking down at the crescent bay.

I pointed to the beach below and said,

"That's where I sat with a piece of simit, wondering if life had anything left for me. And now I'm here... with you."

The Drive to Konya and the Village

From Alanya, we headed inland. The winding mountain roads gave way to open plains.

We entered Konya, the spiritual heart of Turkey—the city of Rumi, of mystics and whirling dervishes. I walked them through the Mevlana Museum, telling them stories of faith and poetry. We walked through the University Campus, and I showed them where I planned the first event with a fashion show. In the evening, we met Bulent and his family for dinner.

Then came the moment I had been carrying in my heart for decades.

We left Konya and drove eastward—toward the village. The land grew dry. The trees grew sparse.

The horizon turned still. So far, our hearts were already swollen with memories — but nothing could prepare me for the weight I felt as we drove into the hills of Sarıkaya. The road narrowed as we approached the village. The air smelled different—like dust and thyme, like summer sweat and sorrow.

I had been here before—too many times in my dreams and once in real life when I was still a boy trying to understand what death really meant. But this was the first time as a father. This time, I wasn't alone. My wife sat beside me in the passenger seat, holding my hand without saying a word. My children were quiet in the back, sensing the shift in the air. This wasn't a sightseeing stop. This was sacred.

We parked near the small cemetery just beyond the hill from the apart hotel and the gas station. I stepped out first and stood still. My knees trembled.

"I need a moment," I told them. But they didn't stay behind. One by one, they followed me, not because I asked but because they knew this mattered.

The cemetery was simple. No grand marble stones. No manicured lawns. Just a humble stretch of land where the wind always seemed to whisper. I walked slowly, my feet knowing exactly where to go. And then, there it was.

His grave.

I dropped to my knees. The dirt looked dry, but to me, it was still wet with the tears I had cried the day we buried him. I touched the cold headstone, gently brushed off some dust, and whispered:

"Baba… I'm here."

The words cracked out of me like thunder. My voice broke. My chest shook. I sobbed without shame. All these years, I had spoken to him in silence. In dreams. In prayers. But now, he could hear me through the air that carried my breath.

And then, I turned.

"Come," I said to my family.

Karla walked over and knelt beside me. She placed her hand on the stone as if to say, Thank you for your son. My daughter stood behind her, tears quietly slipping down her cheek. My older son held his little brother's hand, and both were unsure of what to say, knowing this was bigger than them.

"This is your grandfather," I told them. "The man who gave everything so I could stand where I stand. You never met him… but he's the reason you exist. He's the reason we live in freedom. In comfort. In peace."

I placed my hand on my chest and added, "He never made it to America, but everything I built there has his fingerprints."

I introduced them one by one.

"Baba, this is Karla—the love of my life. You would have loved her. She has my mother's strength and your fire in her eyes.

"This is your granddaughter… so smart, so full of life. She loves to write—maybe one day she'll write about you.

"This is your grandson—he carries your name. And this little one… he's the reason I work even harder."

We stood there for a long time. My daughter placed a small flower she had picked beside the headstone. My sons said nothing, but I saw it in their eyes—they understood. Legacy doesn't need words.

Before we left, I whispered one final thing, my forehead resting against the cool stone:

"I'm okay now, Baba. We're okay. I kept going. Just like you told me to. And I brought them home to you."

Then we walked away slowly, the sun beginning to dip behind the hills—the same hills that once watched over a barefoot boy chasing his father's shadow. Only now, the shadow stood beside me, proud.

We drove a few minutes farther into the village where my mother once waited at the well, where the call to prayer echoed across dust roads, where I once stared at the stars as a boy wondering how I'd ever escape.

We found the house or what was left of it.

A shell. Broken bricks. A roof caved in. Grass growing through the kitchen floor. Time had reclaimed it.

But in that ruin, I saw life. I saw my sisters milking the cow. My grandmother boiling tea. My brothers chasing goats. My grandfather's quiet smile.

Then we drove down to the old gas station my father had built with his own hands—long since sold by my uncles to cover debts.

The three-floor apartment hotel we once dreamed of running—it was gone too. Sold. Lost. Sacrificed to clean up what should have never been broken.

I explained it gently to my children.

That sometimes, in life, people make mistakes.

But no matter what, you must always protect your name, honor, and soul.

And if something is taken from you, you don't live bitter—you build better.

The Final Stop – City of Ankara

From the village, we made our way to Ankara.

We stayed with my mom, visited my brother, and recharged before heading back. I shared childhood stories as we walked the streets where I once begged to be taken back to Hengelo... how I once sold water in the Bazaar here—how I found my fight in this city, and how I became a protector for my brothers and sisters, and where I ultimately learned to stand tall. I showed them the dorm where I lived and the venues I modeled.

Home Again – But Changed

Then, we flew back to Chicago.

But we weren't the same family that had boarded the plane weeks before.

We were different. More connected. More grounded.

As I stepped back into my home, I looked around—at the walls I built, the company I saved, the family I loved—and I realized:

I had finally completed the journey.

From the boy in the orange van

To the man behind the wheel of Infinity.

From a broken village

To a global vision.

From survival

To legacy.

And now, as I sit here writing these final words, I leave this story behind for my children—and for yours:

Don't be afraid to begin with nothing.

Don't be ashamed to cry.

Don't ever forget where you came from.

And never, ever stop moving forward.

Because sometimes…

the van you remember from childhood

is still driving you

all the way home.

Sometimes, while driving down a long stretch of highway, I'll spot one of our Infinity buses up ahead — and for a moment, it feels like the orange van is leading me, showing the way, just like it did when I was a child.

Other times, I see one in my rearview mirror, trailing quietly behind me — as if the orange van is still watching my back, never letting me fall.

And then there are days when I'm completely surrounded—one Infinity bus ahead of me, one behind, and one on each side. In those rare moments, I feel it deeply…as if a powerful circle has formed around me—a shield of motion, memory, and meaning—the spirit of the orange van protecting me from all sides.

So, if you ever find yourself in Chicago — whether for business, for joy or just passing through—and you spot one of our Infinity buses with the orange logo, know this:

You've just crossed paths with the boy in the orange van.

And that boy? He never stopped driving forward.

The Final Words

I didn't just chase the American Dream.

I caught it.

With blistered hands, a heart full of stories, and my father's voice echoing in every step, I built it from the gravel up.

This country didn't give me anything for free, but it gave me a chance.

And that was enough.

So, to every immigrant, dreamer, fighter, and forgotten kid who still believes they're meant for something more — keep going. Keep driving.

Even if your van is rusty. Even if no one believes in you yet.

Because one day, your story might be the one someone sees rolling down the highway, wrapped in orange, wrapped in faith, and impossible to ignore.